LawExpress
EMPLOYMENT LAW

Tried and tested

Law Express has been helping UK law students to revise since 2009 and its power is proven. A recent survey[*] shows that:

- **94%** think that Law Express helps them to revise effectively and take exams with confidence.
- **88%** agree Law Express helps them to understand key concepts quickly.

Individual students attest to how the series has supported their revision:

'Law Express are my go-to guides. They are an excellent supplement to my course material.'
Claire Turner, Open University

'In the modules in which I used these books to revise, generally the modules I found the most difficult, I got the highest marks. The books are really easy to use and are extremely helpful.'
Charlotte Evans, Queen Mary University of London

'The information is straight to the point. This is important particularly for exams.'
Dewan Sadia Kuraishy, University of Manchester

'These revision guides strike the right balance between enough detail to help shape a really good answer, but brief enough to be used for last-minute revision. The layout is user friendly and the use of tables and flowcharts is helpful.'
Shannon Reynolds, University of Manchester

'I personally found the series very helpful in my preparation for exams.'
Abba Elgujja, University of Salford

*A survey of 16 UK law students in September 2014.

EMPLOYMENT LAW

Law Express

5th edition

David Cabrelli

Senior Lecturer in Commercial Law, University of Edinburgh, and a qualified solicitor in Scotland

PEARSON

Harlow, England • London • New York • Boston • San Francisco • Toronto • Sydney • Auckland • Singapore • Hong Kong
Tokyo • Seoul • Taipei • New Delhi • Cape Town • São Paulo • Mexico City • Madrid • Amsterdam • Munich • Paris • Milan

Pearson Education Limited
Edinburgh Gate
Harlow CM20 2JE
United Kingdom
Tel: +44 (0)1279 623623
Web: www.pearson.com/uk

First published 2008 (print)
Second edition published 2010 (print and electronic)
Third edition published 2013 (print and electronic)
Fourth edition published 2015 (print and electronic)
Fifth edition published 2017 (print and electronic)

ISBN: 978-1-292-08682-8 (print)
       978-1-292-08732-0 (PDF)
       978-1-292-08731-3 (ePub)

British Library Cataloguing-in-Publication Data
A catalogue record for the print edition is available from the British Library

10 9 8 7 6 5 4 3 2 1
21 20 19 18 17

Front cover bestseller data from Nielsen BookScan (2009–2014, Law Revision Series).
Back cover poll data from a survey of 16 UK law students in September 2014.

Print edition typeset in 10/12 and Helvetica Neue LT W1G 57 Condensed by Lumina Datamatics, Inc.
Printed by Ashford Colour Press Ltd, Gosport

NOTE THAT ANY PAGE CROSS REFERENCES REFER TO THE PRINT EDITION

Contents

What do you think of LawExpress?

We're really keen to hear your opinions about the series and how well it supports your studies. Your views will help inform the future development of Law Express and ensure it is best suited to the revision needs of law students.

Please log on to the website and leave us your feedback. It will only take a few minutes and your thoughts are invaluable to us.

www.pearsoned.co.uk/lawexpressfeedback

Dedication and acknowledgements

I would like to dedicate this book to my mother, Rosanna Cabrelli. Thanks go to Hannah Marston, Christine Statham, Donna Goddard, Tim Parker, Lauren Hayward, Natasha Whelan, Sue Gard, Zoë Botterill and Katherine Cowdrey at Pearson for their patience and encouragement. The feedback of the anonymous reviewers of the draft chapters was also most helpful and I would like to thank them. In addition, the universities of Edinburgh and Dundee and their students offered excellent insights into certain aspects of employment law which are covered in this book.

David Cabrelli

Author's acknowledgements

Our thanks go to all reviewers who contributed to the development of this text, including students who participated in research and focus groups which helped to shape the series format.

Publisher's acknowledgements

We are grateful to the following for permission to reproduce copyright material:

Figures 11.1 and 11.2 from HMSO, Contains public sector information licensed under the Open Government Licence (OGL) v3.0. http://www.nationalarchives.gov.uk/doc/open-government-licence.

In some instances we have been unable to trace the owners of copyright material, and we would appreciate any information that would enable us to do so.

Introduction

Employment law is an optional subject which students may take as part of a qualifying undergraduate law degree. Although it is optional, it is extremely popular. Students who choose to take employment law find it very interesting and are often engaged by the breadth of coverage of the topics comprising the subject. This, together with the fact that employment law is a growth area in legal practice and that more and more solicitors specialise in this area of law, means that its popularity and appeal among students is likely to be guaranteed for many years to come.

Employment is an integral part of everyday life. It is a prominent feature in the news and media. Indeed, one of the advantages of studying a subject such as employment law is that many students are also (or have been) employees and are able to conceptualise and connect with many of the topics which are covered. For example, most students will have a basic understanding of what is meant by redundancy, dismissal and discrimination. The contrast with concepts such as 'easements' and 'adverse possession' in land law is stark.

Employment law is statute based and case law based. The most important statutes are the Employment Rights Act 1996, the Trade Union and Labour Relations (Consolidation) Act 1992 and the Equality Act 2010. Employment law is an extremely dynamic area of law and changes very quickly. During your studies, there are likely to be a number of key changes in the law.

This revision guide will help you to identify and apply the law. Its objective is to provide frequent reminders of the importance of understanding the legal definitions of key employment law concepts, such as 'redundancy', 'dismissal', 'trade union', 'direct discrimination' and many others. It is written to be used as a supplement to your course materials, lectures and textbooks. As a revision guide, it should do just that – guide you through revision; it should not be used to cut down on the amount of reading (or thinking) that you have to do in order to succeed. Employment law is a vast, complex and dynamic subject – you should realise this from looking at the size of your recommended textbook. It follows that this revision guide could never be expected to cover the subject in the depth and detail required to succeed in exams and it does not set out to do so. Instead, it aims to provide a concise overall picture of the key areas for revision – reminding you of the headline points to enable you to focus your revision and identify the key points that you need to know.

📖 REVISION NOTE

- Do not be misled by the familiarity of the terminology; ensure that you learn each topic afresh and focus on the legal meanings of the words that you encounter.
- Do rely on this book to guide you through the revision process.
- Do not rely on this book to tell you everything that you need to know about employment law – that is the job of your lecturer's recommended textbook.
- Make sure you consult your own syllabus frequently to check which topics are covered and in how much detail.
- Make use of your lecture notes, handouts, textbooks and other materials as you revise as these will ensure that you have sufficient depth of knowledge.
- Take every possible opportunity to practise your essay-writing and problem-solving technique; get as much feedback as you can.
- Be aware that many questions in employment law combine different topics. Selective revision could leave you unable to answer questions which include reference to material that you have excluded from your revision.

Before you begin, you can use the study plan available on the companion website to assess how well you know the material in this book and identify the areas where you may want to focus your revision.

Guided tour

Topic maps – Visual guides highlight key subject areas and facilitate easy navigation through the chapter. Download them from the companion website to pin on your wall or add to your revision notes.

Revision checklists – How well do you know each topic? Use these to identify essential points you should know for your exams. But don't panic if you don't know them all – the chapters will help you revise each point to ensure you are fully prepared. Print the checklists off the companion website and track your revision progress!

Sample questions with answer guidelines – Practice makes perfect! Read the question at the start of each chapter and consider how you would answer it. Guidance on structuring strong answers is provided at the end of the chapter. Try out additional sample questions online.

Assessment advice – Not sure how best to tackle a problem or essay question? Wondering what you may be asked? Use the assessment advice to identify the ways in which a subject may be examined and how to apply your knowledge effectively.

Key definitions – Make sure you understand essential legal terms. Use the flashcards online to test your recall!

Key cases and key statutes – Identify and review the important elements of the essential cases and statutes you will need to know for your exams.

Make your answer stand out – This feature illustrates sources of further thinking and debate where you can maximise your marks. Use them to really impress your examiners!

Exam tips – Feeling the pressure? These boxes indicate how you can improve your exam performance when it really counts.

Revision notes – Get guidance for effective revision. These boxes highlight related points and areas of overlap in the subject, or areas where your course might adopt a particular approach that you should check with your course tutor.

Don't be tempted to... – This feature underlines areas where students most often trip up in exams. Use them to spot common pitfalls and avoid losing marks.

Read to impress – Focus on these carefully selected sources to extend your knowledge, deepen your understanding, and earn better marks in coursework as well as in exams.

Glossary – Forgotten the meaning of a word? This quick reference covers key definitions and other useful terms.

Table of cases and statutes

Cases

■ Statutes

TABLE OF CASES AND STATUTES

▉ Statutory Instruments

■ European Legislation

Conventions and Treaties

Directives

The sources and institutions of employment law and key definitions

1

Revision checklist

Essential points you should know:

- [ ] The sources of employment law
- [ ] The institutions of employment law
- [ ] Distinction between an 'employee' and an 'independent contractor'
- [ ] An understanding of the 'worker' and 'contract personally to do work' categories
- [ ] Relationship between each of the categories

■ Topic map

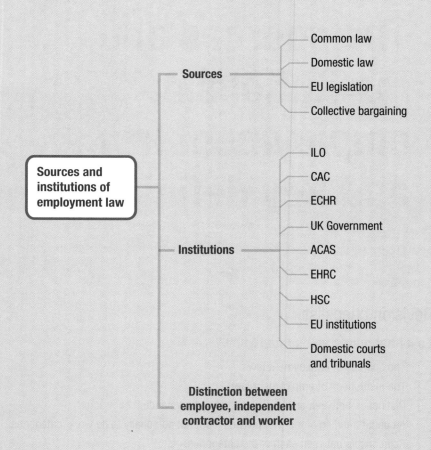

■ Introduction

Employment law has a number of sources and specific institutions and employment rights are available to employees, workers and independent contractors who have entered into a 'contract personally to do work'.

Exam questions that ask students to determine whether an individual is an employee or an independent contractor are common and so this chapter will equip you with the tools to answer such a question confidently. There are three sections to this chapter:

- the sources of employment law;
- the institutions of employment law;
- an analysis of the concepts of 'employee', 'worker' and independent contractors who have entered into contracts 'personally to do work'.

ASSESSMENT ADVICE

Essay questions

In connection with the sources and institutions of employment law, essay questions require broad general knowledge of those sources and institutions and their effect on the development of employment law and the enforcement of employment rights. You will also be expected to explain how legislation and the common law define the key concepts of 'employee', 'worker' and the 'contract personally to do work'. An understanding of key cases in respect of each of these concepts is required. You must also exhibit knowledge of the employment rights enjoyed by 'employees', 'workers' and certain categories of self-employed persons. In tackling essay questions, you should always directly answer the question(s) asked and apply the relevant law.

Problem questions

Concentrating on the sources and institutions of employment law, problem questions may be framed in such a way that you are asked to advise employees regarding the source of the rights available to them (e.g. rights based on domestic legislation, rights enshrined in domestic legislation which are based on EU law, rights having EU law directly as their source) and the competing prospects of success in raising a claim based on these sources in an employment tribunal, or a legal action in the courts. Most problem questions on the concepts of 'employee' and 'worker' will involve an examination of a person's relationship with an enterprise and whether that person amounts to an 'employee' working under a contract of employment, a ▶

'worker' or an independent contractor who has entered into a 'contract personally to do work'. In answering problem questions, you will need to discuss the relevant statutory definitions and common law tests which distinguish between these categories. This may also be combined with other areas of employment law (e.g. if the person is a 'worker', what employment rights do they enjoy). In tackling problem questions, you should always directly answer the question(s) asked and apply the relevant law to the facts at hand.

■ Sample question

Could you answer this question? Below is a typical essay question that could arise on this topic. Guidelines on answering the question are included at the end of the chapter, while a sample problem question and guidance on tackling it can be found on the companion website.

ESSAY QUESTION

Analyse how the law distinguishes between persons working under a contract of service and independent contractors. What is the legal significance of this distinction and is the law in need of reform?

■ Sources of employment law

With the exception of Chapter 11, this revision guide is concerned with the individual rights of **employees**, **workers** and independent contractors who have entered into contracts '*personally to do work*' – which are directly enforceable against employers. The sources of employment law and employment rights are diverse. The topic map outlines the key (but not all) sources of individual employment law. One of the most important sources is EU law. EU law provides employees, workers and certain self-employed persons/independent contractors with employment rights directly enforceable in the UK courts and tribunals via the Treaty on the Functioning of the European Union, EU regulations and the decisions of the Court of Justice of the European Union. EU Directives provide employment rights directly in the national courts when domestic legislation implementing the terms of a Directive has come into force.

■ Institutions of employment law

There are a number of distinctive institutions of employment law. Some are designed to enforce employment rights and resolve employment disputes, such as the domestic courts, Employment Tribunals, the Employment Appeal Tribunal, the Central Arbitration Committee (CAC), the European Court of Human Rights (ECtHR) and the Court of Justice of the European Union. Others are intended to act as institutions that prevent such disputes arising in the first place, such as the Advisory, Conciliation and Arbitration Service (ACAS) and the Equality and Human Rights Commission (EHRC). Some act as standard-setters, such as the International Labour Organization (ILO) and ACAS (Codes of Practice), while others act as rule-makers, such as the European Parliament, the Council of the European Union and the UK Government. (See the topic map.)

Employment tribunals and the Employment Appeal Tribunal

Specific mention must be made of the Employment Tribunals (ETs) and the Employment Appeal Tribunal (EAT). ETs are specialist tribunals comprising one qualified lawyer and two laypersons. One layperson is selected after consultation with employers' organisations. The other layperson is appointed after consultation with **trade unions**. The ETs are tribunals and are designed to be informal and cheaper for the public to use than domestic courts. ETs resolve disputes about employment rights which have legislation as their source. However, there are limited rights to raise employment claims before the ET where the dispute has the common law as its source. The constitutional basis and procedures of ETs are contained within the Employment Tribunals (Constitution and Rules of Procedure) Regulations 2013 and the Employment Appeal Tribunal Fees Order 2013. Meanwhile, the EAT is composed of divisions with hearings taking place in London or Edinburgh. The EAT is staffed with judges of the High Court in England or Senators of the College of Justice in the Court of Session in Scotland. Such judges or Senators must have experience or an understanding of employment law and employment relations. The EAT hears appeals from the ETs on points of employment law, *inter alia*. See Figure 1.1 for a flowchart of the channel of appeals and how an Article 267 referral for a preliminary ruling may be made to the Court of Justice of the European Union (CJEU, formerly the European Court of Justice, ECJ).

Figure 1.1

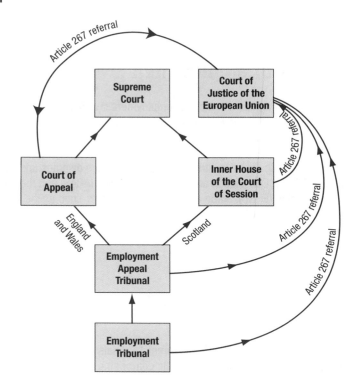

◼ Distinction between an 'employee', 'worker' and 'independent contractor'

'Employees' are entitled to the full suite of common law and statutory employment rights. 'Workers' and certain categories of self-employed persons/independent contractors enjoy varying degrees of limited employment rights.

Is an individual an 'employee'?

The courts have developed a number of tests to distinguish an 'employee' from an independent contractor.

KEY STATUTE

Employment Rights Act 1996 (ERA 1996), s. 230(1) and the Trade Union and Labour Relations (Consolidation) Act 1992 (TULRCA 1992), s. 295(1)

An 'employee' is 'an individual who has entered into or works under. . .a contract of employment'.

KEY STATUTE

ERA 1996, s. 230(2) and TULRCA 1992, s. 295(1)

In this Act 'contract of employment' means a 'contract of service. . .whether express or implied and (if it is express) whether oral or in writing'.

Common law tests for establishing 'contract of service'

No further statutory guidance is provided as to how the courts determine whether a 'contract of service' exists. Hence, the common law has established a number of tests in order to ascertain whether an individual is undertaking work on the basis of a contract of employment:

- The 'integration' test. Here, the courts enquire whether the work of the individual is an integral part of the business or organisation of the employer. If the answer is yes, then this is a factor in favour of the individual being an employee. See *Stevenson, Jordan and Harrison Ltd* v *Macdonald and Evans* (1952).
- The 'economic reality' test. This involves asking whether the individual is not working for his own account. If the answer is yes, this is a factor in favour of the individual being an employee. See *Market Investigations Ltd* v *Minister of Social Security* (1969).
- The 'mutuality of obligation' test. Here, one asks whether there is an obligation on the part of the enterprise to provide a minimum or reasonable amount of work to the individual and pay for it and whether there is a corresponding obligation on the individual to undertake a minimum or reasonable amount of work. If the answer is yes, then this is a factor in favour of the individual being an employee. See *Carmichael and Leese* v *National Power plc* (1999).
- The 'control' test:

KEY CASE

Ready Mixed Concrete (South East) Ltd v *Minister of Pensions and National Insurance* [1968] 1 All ER 433

Concerning: contract of employment, 'control' test

Facts

A yardman batcher entered into a new contract with a company which made and sold concrete. The contract involved the carriage of concrete and a dispute emerged regarding the status of the individual.

Legal principle

In order for a contract of service to exist, each of the following must be present:

(1) the individual must provide his own work and exercise skill in the performance of his work in return for wages or other remuneration;

(2) the individual must subject himself to the control of the other to a sufficient degree; and

(3) the other provisions of the contract must be consistent with a contract of service.

(4) As for the meaning of 'control', it includes the power of deciding the thing to be done, the way in which it shall be done, the means to be employed in doing it, the time when, and the place where it shall be done.

The 'multiple' test

In coming to a view as to whether an individual is an employee, the courts and tribunals now apply a 'mixed/multiple' test: *Ready Mixed Concrete (South East) Ltd* v *Minister of Pensions and National Insurance* (1968). In other words, they take into account each of the above four tests and a number of other factors. The greater the number of tests which have been satisfied and the greater the number of factors present, the more likely it is that the individual will be an employee. The relevant factors are as follows:

■ Does the contract give the individual no absolute right to send along a substitute to provide the work? If the answer is yes, then the more likely it is that the individual is an employee.

■ Is the individual paid wages or a salary rather than a fee, commission or royalties? If yes, then the more likely it is that the individual is an employee.

■ Has the individual invested no capital in his work and does he suffer no risk of loss? If yes, then the more likely it is that the individual is an employee.

■ Does the enterprise provide the individual's tools, uniform, stationery, equipment or materials? If yes, then the more likely it is that the individual is an employee.

■ Does the individual pay income tax and NICs as an employee rather than charge VAT on his services or pay income tax and NICs as an independent contractor? If the latter, then the more likely it is that the individual is an employee.

■ Does the enterprise have the power to suspend, discipline or dismiss the individual or initiate or respond to disciplinary or grievance procedures? If yes, then the more likely it is that the individual is an employee.

■ What label have the parties attached to their relationship? This will not be definitive, but may be relevant in a borderline case – see *Massey* v *Crown Life Insurance Co.* (1978).

Basic ingredients for contract of employment

Although the courts and tribunals apply the multiple test, what is clear is that if any one of the following three criteria are absent, then the courts will hold that the individual concerned is not an employee:

■ control;

■ mutuality of obligation;

■ a degree of personal service on the part of the individual providing services.

The above three factors represent the 'irreducible minimum criteria' (i.e. the basic ingredients) which the courts require to be present.

KEY CASE

Montgomery v *Johnson Underwood Ltd* [2001] IRLR 269

Concerning: contract of employment, basic ingredients

Facts

Montgomery was registered as an agency worker with Johnson Underwood (the agency) and was placed with a client company of the agency. There was a dispute as to whether the agency or the client company was her employer.

Legal principle

Montgomery was not the employee of the agency or the client company. The Court of Appeal held that 'mutuality of obligation' and 'control' represented the irreducible minimum required for the establishment of a contract of employment. The fact that there was insufficient control on the part of the agency in this case meant that Montgomery could not be their employee.

KEY CASE

Carmichael and Leese v *National Power plc* **[1999] 4 All ER 897, [2000] IRLR 43**

Concerning: the status of 'casual – as required' workers

Facts

On the basis of a letter, Carmichael was appointed as a tour guide on a 'casual – as required basis'. There were no set hours of work and payment was made at an hourly rate for work actually done, after deduction of income tax and national insurance. After a period of time, Carmichael argued that she was an employee.

Legal principle

Taking into account the terms of the letter, the oral exchanges between the parties, the surrounding circumstances and the subsequent conduct of the parties, it was clear that there was no mutuality of obligation present in the relationship. Accordingly, Mrs Carmichael was not an employee. The arrangement between the parties was flexible in that there was no intention to create an employment relationship which subsisted when Mrs Carmichael was not working.

Atypical workers

In the past 30 years, businesses have demanded and obtained more and more flexibility in the labour market. Organisations are keen to hire intermittent labour to meet market demands and offload labour as cheaply as possible when it is no longer required. *Carmichael* demonstrates the issues which can arise when an individual providing work to an organisation is an 'atypical' worker. A typical worker can be defined as someone who provides work:

- on the basis of a permanent contract;
- for a single, identifiable employer;
- at that employer's premises;
- regardless of whether the employer has work or no work to provide.

In the case of an atypical worker, one of these four criteria is missing. Atypical workers come in a variety of shapes and sizes:

- casual workers – who are engaged to provide work like Carmichael on a 'zero-hours' or a 'freelance' basis. Such workers may be asked to provide work only when the organisation requires them. When there is no work, they take the risk of the shortage of work;
- agency workers like Montgomery who are hired out to a client company via an employment agency;
- fixed-term workers (e.g. seasonal workers employed on short-term contracts);

- part-time workers;
- homeworkers (who work at home).

The main difficulty with atypical workers is that they are often dependent workers in a position of subordination vis-à-vis the organisation that engages them to provide work. However, they are more often than not unlikely to be held by the courts and/or tribunals to be employees by virtue of the absence of any mutuality of obligation or control.

! Don't be tempted to . . .

You should not fall into the trap of thinking that the Agency Workers' Regulations 2010 (SI 2010/93) clarify whether the agency worker is an employee of the employment agency or the hiring company. By virtue of regulation 5 of the Agency Workers' Regulations, when agency workers are hired by an employment agency to a hiring company, they are given the right not to be treated less favourably than the permanent employees or workers of the hiring company in respect of the pay-related terms and conditions of their contract. Hence, these provisions ensure parity of pay-related contractual terms and conditions. However, in order for the agency worker to be deemed an employee of the hiring company, the common law test in *James* v *London Borough of Greenwich* (2008) will continue to apply, namely whether it is *necessary* to imply a contract of employment between the agency worker and the hiring company. Given that there will often be a contract for services in place between the agency worker and the employment agency it will be extremely difficult for the agency worker to satisfy this necessity test.

✎ EXAM TIP

In an essay question or problem question, look out for any assertion that the individual has no contractual obligation to accept an offer of work from an organisation – or that an organisation has no absolute obligation to offer a minimum or reasonable amount of work to an individual. Here, you should be discussing the 'mutuality of obligation' criterion, what this means and the legal implications of its absence. However, where the question refers to such a 'no obligations' clause in the individual's contract with the hirer, but goes on to say that neither of the parties have ever relied on this clause, you should be mindful of the exposition of the 'sham' doctrine in the decision of the Supreme Court in *Autoclenz Ltd* v *Belcher* (2011). In *Autoclenz*, the Supreme Court ruled that where the written terms of the contract between the parties fail to reflect their true relationship, and the hirer is operating at a higher level of bargaining strength, the courts and tribunals will be prepared to look at the situation on the ground in order to set aside the written terms of the contract, i.e. to treat them as a 'sham' and hold that the individual is an employee.

Is an individual a 'worker'?

If an individual is not an employee, then they are likely to be an independent contractor. However, before coming to this conclusion, it is appropriate to consider whether they are a 'worker', since persons falling within this category will enjoy the employment rights listed in Figure 1.2.

Figure 1.2

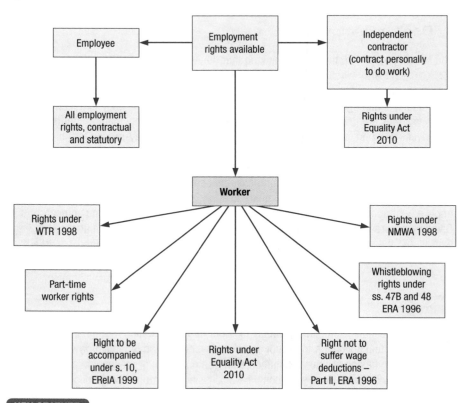

KEY STATUTE

ERA 1996, s. 230(3), National Minimum Wage Act 1998, s. 54(3) and the Working Time Regulations 1998, reg. 1

In this Act 'worker' means an individual who has entered into or works under. . .(a) a contract of employment, or (b) any other contract. . .whereby the individual undertakes to do or perform personally any work or services for another party to the contract whose status is not by virtue of the contract that of a client or customer of any profession or business undertaking carried on by the individual.

The key components of the 'worker' contract

In order to constitute a 'worker', an individual providing services to another must show the following four factors:

- the presence of mutuality of obligation;
- personal service on the part of the individual providing the services to another which must be the dominant feature of the contract – see *James* v *Redcats (Brands) Ltd* (2007) and *Clyde & Co. LLP* v *Bates van Winkelhof* (2014);
- the recipient of the services must not be the client or customer of the individual providing the services.

⊓ REVISION NOTE

It is clear that the presence of 'mutuality of obligation' lies at the heart of the existence of both an employment contract and a 'worker' contract.

Is the individual an independent contractor who enjoys certain limited employment rights?

If an individual is neither an 'employee' nor a 'worker', then they are an independent contractor. However, this does not mean that they enjoy no employment rights at all. Certain self-employed persons who enter into contracts 'personally to do work' do have the benefit of certain employment rights: for example, the anti-discrimination and equal pay rights under the Equality Act 2010.

KEY STATUTE

Equality Act 2010, s. 83(2)

'Employment' means employment under a contract of service. . .or *a contract personally to do work. . .*' [emphasis added]

KEY CASE

Mingeley v *Pennock and Ivory t/a Amber Cars* [2004] IRLR 373

Concerning: 'contract personally to do work'

Facts

Mingeley was of black African origin. He worked as a private-hire taxi driver; he owned the car he used for that purpose. By contract with Amber Cars, he paid £75.00 a week ▶

for access to its radio and computer system, which allocated calls to drivers. He kept the fares he collected. The Race Relations Act 1976 conferred anti-discrimination rights on the ground of race in favour of an individual who entered into a 'contract personally to execute any work or labour'. The question was whether Mingeley satisfied this definition.

Legal principle

The Court of Appeal held that for a person to be employed under a contract personally to execute any work or labour there required to be mutual obligations to offer or accept work. Since this was not present, Mingeley did not satisfy the definition in section 78(1) of the Race Relations Act 1976. The same reasoning applies to the 'contract personally to do work', which is found in the definition of 'employment' in section 83(2) of the Equality Act 2010.

The nature of the 'worker' contract and the 'contract personally to do work'

What is clear about the definition of the 'worker' and the 'contract personally to do work' is that, like the definition of 'employee', there is a requirement for:

- mutuality of obligation;
- the individual concerned must personally provide a service to another under the direction of that other person in return for which the individual receives remuneration, with personal service being the dominant feature of the contract: *Jivraj* v *Hashwani* (2011).

Three points can be made here:

- For an individual to be engaged on the basis of a 'contract personally to do work', the subordination of that individual to the hirer of his/her services must be a dominant feature of the contract: *Jivraj* v *Hashwani* (2011).
- If a contract gives the individual the *absolute* power to send along a substitute to perform the work, they will not satisfy the definitions of 'worker' and 'contract personally to do work' – see *Community Dental Centres Ltd* v *Sultan-Darmon* (2010).
- The coverage of the 'contract personally to do work' is wider than the 'worker' contract. In the case of the latter, one must enquire whether the recipient of the individual's services is a client or customer of the individual concerned. This means that individuals providing services personally to clients or customers are not covered. In contrast, in the case of the 'contract personally to do work', the individual concerned may be providing services personally to clients or customers – yet be covered by the legislation.

Make your answer stand out

Commentators in favour of restructuring the employment relationship and moving away from the model of the contract of employment advocate a codified structure – akin to status over contract, e.g. Hepple (1986). On the other side of the debate are those who favour the retention of the existing contractual model, albeit in a (radically) reformed guise. For example, Freedland is of the view that employment law should continue to be predicated on contract law. Students who consider whether the employment relationship ought to continue to be based on the law of contract would be going above and beyond what is asked and are likely to gain additional marks. The articles by Hepple (1986) and Freedland (2006) in the 'Read to Impress' box below are useful reading.

■ Putting it all together

Answer guidelines

See the essay question at the start of this chapter. A diagram illustrating how to structure your answer is available on the website.

Approaching the question

There are three elements to this question and it is critical that you deal with each in turn in your answer. If you deal with the first and the third, but not the second element (or vice versa), you are likely to lose at least one-third of the marks allocated to the question. See below for details of those three elements.

Important points to include

Points to remember when answering this question:

■ An introduction should be included which explains the changes in the structure of the underlying labour market and economy over the past 40 years and the shift away from the permanent and rigid 'standard employment relationship' towards atypical working relationships.

■ Differentiate between the contract of employment, the contract for services, the 'worker' contract and the 'contract personally to do work'.

►

- Address the various tests which are applied, and have been applied, by the courts to determine the status of an individual providing services. What are the minimum criteria which must be present for the existence of a contract of employment?

 Make your answer stand out

- Address the academic debates regarding the appropriateness of the contractual model at the heart of the employment relationship, the 'worker' contract and the 'contract personally to do work'.
- Explore the possible path and future development of the employment relationship. Is the law flexible enough to cater for atypical working relationships?

READ TO IMPRESS

Collins, H. (1986) Market power, bureaucratic power, and the contract of employment. 15 *Industrial Law Journal*: 1.

Deakin, S. (2007) Does the 'Personal Employment Contract' provide a basis for the reunification of employment law? 36(1) *Industrial Law Journal*: 68.

Freedland, M. (2006) From the contract of employment to the personal work nexus. 35(1) *Industrial Law Journal*: 1.

Freedland, M. and Kountouris, N. (2008) Towards a comparative theory of the contractual construction of personal work relations in Europe. 37(1) *Industrial Law Journal*: 5.

Hepple, B. (1986) Restructuring employment rights. 15 *Industrial Law Journal*: 69.

Kahn-Freund, O. (1967) A note on status and contract in British labour law. 30 *Modern Law Review*: 635.

Leighton, P. and Wynn, M. (2011) Classifying employment relationships – more sliding doors or a better regulatory framework? 40 *Industrial Law Journal*: 5.

www.pearsoned.co.uk/lawexpress

 Go online to access more revision support including quizzes to test your knowledge, sample questions with answer guidelines, podcasts you can download, and more!

Implied terms of the contract of employment (1): duties of the employer

2

Revision checklist

Essential points you should know:

- [ ] The different types of implied duties imposed on an employer
- [ ] The sources of the implied duties
- [ ] The circumstances under which an employer will be in breach of duty in failing to provide an employee with work
- [ ] The different types of sub-duties imposed on an employer pursuant to the overall duty to exercise reasonable care
- [ ] The content, nature and scope of the employer's duty to maintain trust and confidence

■ Topic map

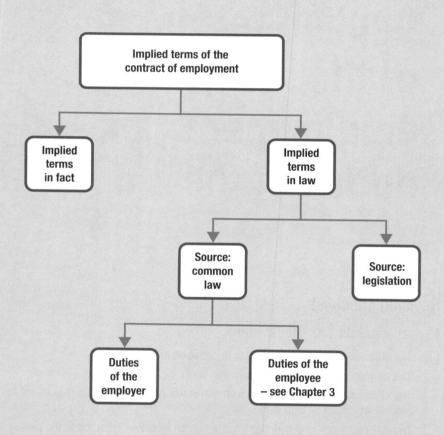

A printable version of this topic map is available from **www.pearsoned.co.uk/lawexpress**

■ Introduction

By operation of law, an employer owes a number of diverse implied duties to an employee.

This chapter concentrates on the implied terms of the contract of employment. The implied terms of the contract of employment can be divided into (1) those implied terms which can be seen as imposing implied duties on an employer in favour of an employee and (2) those implied terms which can be viewed as imposing implied duties on an employee in favour of the employer. In Chapter 2 we will concentrate on the employer's implied duties and in Chapter 3 we will consider the employee's implied duties.

The implied duties arise by operation of law by virtue of the fact that the employer and employee have entered into a contract of employment. For this reason, the implied terms in law can be distinguished from implied terms in fact. Implied terms in law are implied into every contract of employment. However, implied terms in fact are not implied into every contract of employment as a matter of law, but are case-specific implied terms which are introduced into a contract of employment in a particular case in order to give it 'business efficacy'.

The sources of the implied duties are (i) the common law and (ii) legislation. However, some of the implied duties having the common law as their source have been influenced by legislation.

ASSESSMENT ADVICE

Essay questions

These require broad general knowledge of the implied duties of the employer. In particular, the examiner may be looking for an examination of the development of the implied duties and whether the current position is satisfactory. In addressing the broader aspects of the implied duties, the examiner will also expect you to address the sources, content, nature and scope of application of the implied duties. In tackling essay questions, you should always directly answer the question(s) asked and apply the relevant law.

Problem questions

These may involve an examination of more than one of the implied duties of the employer. This may also be combined with other areas of employment law. For example,

▶

- the implied duties of the employee;
- in the case of the employer's implied duty to pay wages/remunerate, the effect on this duty of the National Minimum Wage Act 1998 and the prohibitions on the unauthorised deductions of wages in Part II of the Employment Rights Act 1996 (ERA).

Problem questions concentrating on the implied duties of an employer may be framed in such a way that you will be asked to advise employees whether they have a reasonable prospect of success in raising a claim in an employment tribunal or a legal action in the courts. In tackling problem questions, you should always directly answer the question(s) asked and apply the relevant law to the facts at hand.

Sample question

Could you answer this question? Below is a typical problem question that could arise on this topic. Guidelines on answering the question are included at the end of the chapter, while a sample essay question and guidance on tackling it can be found on the companion website.

PROBLEM QUESTION

Jonathan, a senior engineer, has been employed by an engineering company for seven years and consults you after he was told to go home by his employer at a recent meeting. His employer told him that it had no work to give him and would let him know as soon as work became available. At the meeting, Jonathan was also told by his employer that he would no longer receive the free shares in the employer's company which he had received every month in terms of his written contract of employment. On his way out of the meeting, Jonathan tripped over an unattended bucket of water (which he had not seen) and broke his leg. Advise Jonathan on the rights he enjoys in terms of the implied terms of his contract of employment.

Duty to provide work?

An employer is under no duty to provide an employee with work (e.g. *Turner* v *Sawdon & Co.* (1901) and *Collier* v *Sunday Referee Publishing Co. Ltd* (1940)). However, the courts have created exceptions to this general rule in certain factual circumstances where the nature of the employee's work is so important that the employee requires to work at all times in order to:

- maintain or develop key skill levels (*William Hill Organisation Ltd* v *Tucker* (1998)); or
- keep up to date with developments in the industry, sector or trade within which he works (*Breach* v *Epsylon Industries Ltd* (1976)).

Furthermore, an employer may also be under a duty to provide work where:

- there was an understanding between the employer and employee that the employee would be given a reasonable amount of work in order that he could enjoy a certain level of earnings (*Devonald* v *Rosser* & *Sons* (1906)); or
- the failure to provide the employee with work may lead to a loss of reputation or publicity on the part of the employee (*Herbert Clayton and Jack Waller Ltd* v *Oliver* (1930)).

Much will depend on the facts and circumstances of the case.

Scope of exceptions

Students often find it difficult to understand fully how the exceptions to the general rule apply. Where they apply, the employer is under a duty to provide an employee with work. The exceptions fall broadly within four types: see Figure 2.1 for guidance.

KEY CASE

William Hill Organisation Ltd v *Tucker* **[1998] IRLR 313**

Concerning: duty to provide work, exception

Facts

The employer of a senior dealer in a spread betting business requested that he go on 'garden leave' when the dealer served notice that he was terminating his contract of employment to take up fresh employment with a competitor of the employer. 'Garden leave' describes the situation where an employer requires an employee not to work during the period of notice of termination of employment, subject to the continued receipt of all other contractual benefits, including salary, during that period.

Legal principle

In the case of a highly skilled employee (such as Mr Tucker), in the absence of a clause in the contract of employment, garden leave will not be possible. Accordingly, Mr Tucker was entitled to be provided with work during the notice period. Note that, if the employee had not been highly skilled, this case suggests that the employer would have been able to put him on garden leave, whether or not an express term to that effect had been inserted in his written contract. Meanwhile, in *SG & R Valuation Service Co.* v *Boudrais* (2008) IRLR 770, it was held that where the employee has breached the contract of employment or some other duty such that he/she has rendered it impossible or reasonably impracticable for the employer to provide work, the employer will be entitled to compel the employee to go on garden leave – even in the absence of a garden leave clause.

Figure 2.1

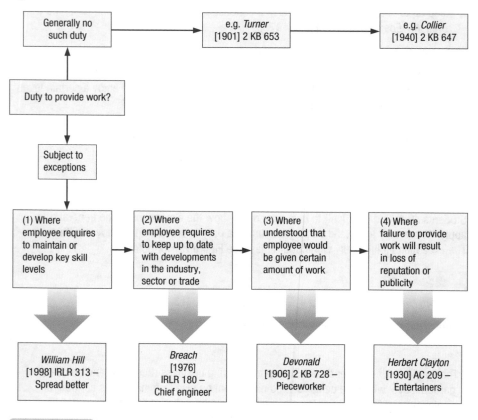

✎ EXAM TIP

In a problem question, look out for an employee who is described as a 'professional', 'salesman', 'engineer', 'entertainer', 'actor' or 'performer'. In such questions, you should immediately think of the exceptions to the general rule.

Duty to pay wages/remunerate when there is no work

Where an employee is not undertaking work, but is ready and willing to work, he will be entitled to be paid and remunerated. However, there are exceptions to this general rule. For example, in the absence of an express term to the contrary, the employer may legally withhold wages:

- where the employer requires to close down a place of business through no fault of its own (e.g. *Browning* v *Crumlin Valley Collieries Ltd* (1926)); or
- an employee is absent owing to ill-health.

In the second case above, the employee remains entitled to statutory sick pay.

Ill health

Complications arise where an employee is absent from work owing to long-term sickness. In terms of social security law, an employee who is ill and absent from work is entitled to be paid statutory sick pay. However, statutory sick pay is capped at a rather low figure. Therefore, the question is whether an employee is entitled to be paid full wages over and above the statutory sick pay. If the contract of employment is silent, the case of *Mears* v *Safecar Security Ltd* (1983) suggests that the answer to this question will be negative, unless the employee can point to some implied term to the contrary.

> ✎ **EXAM TIP**
>
> The area of the payment of wages to and the remuneration of employees is influenced by legislation. First, the National Minimum Wage Act 1998 sets a minimum threshold on the amount of wages which can be paid to employees in a working hour. Secondly, the terms of Part II of the ERA control the extent to which an employer may make unauthorised deductions from the wages of employees. Thirdly, the law of constructive dismissal, in terms of Part X of the ERA, regulates the extent to which an employer can unilaterally vary the express terms of the contract of employment concerning the payment of wages and other contractual benefits. Fourthly, section 28 of the ERA affects the payment of remuneration to employees by conferring statutory guarantee pay in certain circumstances.

▣ Duty in respect of discretionary bonuses

The employer is under an implied duty to exercise a discretion to pay a discretionary bonus in a manner which is bona fide and rational. A refusal to make a discretionary bonus payment will amount to a breach of the implied duty if no employer would have exercised that discretion in that way: that is, the decision was perverse, irrational or contrary to good faith. See *Horkulak* v *Cantor Fitzgerald Ltd* (2004).

▣ Duty to indemnify employee in respect of expenses reasonably incurred

An employee is entitled to be reimbursed by the employer in respect of any costs and expenses the former incurs in performing his employment duties.

Duty to exercise reasonable care for the employee's physical and psychological well-being

An employer is under a duty to exercise reasonable care in respect of the employee's physical and psychological well-being. This duty is a contractual duty, but its content is heavily influenced by the duty of care in negligence in the law of tort and delict (in Scotland). Therefore, whether an employer has breached the implied duty to exercise reasonable care depends on whether the employer has discharged the relevant standard of care and taken the necessary steps. If the employer has not met the requisite standard of care, the court will hold that the implied duty has been breached. Issues of causation, remoteness of damage and quantum will equally be relevant in the law of the contract of employment and in the law of tort or delict (in Scotland). See Figure 2.2 for a breakdown of the relevant stages.

Content and nature of the implied duty

The implied duty to exercise reasonable care can be divided into three sub-duties (see Figure 2.3):

- the employer's duty to provide safe plant, equipment, tools, materials and appliances in the workplace;
- the employer's duty to provide a safe and secure system of work;
- the employer's duty to provide the employee with reasonably competent fellow employees.

KEY CASE

Wilsons & Clyde Coal Co. Ltd v *English* [1938] AC 57

Concerning: duty to exercise reasonable care, physical well-being

Facts

An employee was killed as a result of an accident at work caused by a colleague. The employer argued that the duty to provide a safe system of work had been delegated to the employee's colleague and that it was not liable.

Legal principle

The House of Lords held that the implied duty was personal to the employer. It could not be devolved upon one of its employees. Therefore, the employer could be held liable for negligence in the performance or discharge of that implied duty to exercise reasonable care. Accordingly, the doctrine of 'common employment' was abolished.

Figure 2.2

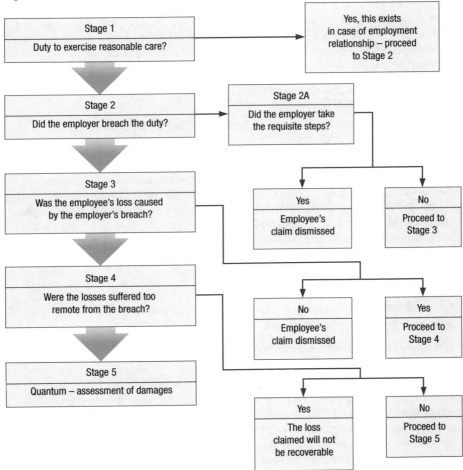

Figure 2.3

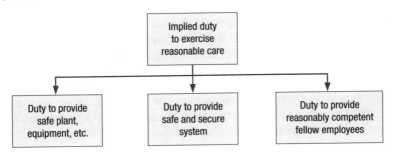

✎ EXAM TIP

In an essay question or problem question, look out for any assertion that there is an express term in the contract of employment to the effect that the weekly working hours of the employee may exceed 48 hours at the option or discretion of the employer. A question like this is looking for you to discuss the following:

1. the extent to which the implied terms of the contract of employment may overrule the express terms of that contract;
2. the effect of regulation 4(1) and (2) of the Working Time Regulations 1998 (SI 1998/1833) on the implied duty.

With regard to 1, in *Johnstone* v *Bloomsbury Health Authority* (1991) it was held that the employer's implied duty to exercise reasonable care may overrule the employer's exercise of discretion based upon the express contractual powers of the employer. In relation to 2, regulation 4(1) of the Working Time Regulations 1998 enables an employee and employer to opt out of the employee's right not to work in excess of 48 hours in a working week. If the employee provides his or her agreement in writing to waive such a right, the agreement is effective. (See Chapter 4 for further details.)

KEY CASE

Johnstone v *Bloomsbury Health Authority* [1991] IRLR 118

Concerning: duty to exercise reasonable care, express terms, psychiatric well-being

Facts

An employee was employed as a junior doctor by a hospital. His written contract of employment provided that his standard working week was 40 hours. However, his employer had discretion to call on him to work an extra 48 hours a week on average. Some weeks, it was alleged, the employee was working in excess of 100 hours. The consequence was that he suffered from stress and depression.

Legal principle

The Court of Appeal held that the employer's implied duty to exercise reasonable care is capable of overruling the employer's exercise of discretion based upon the express contractual powers of the employer. Thus, the exercise of the employer's option to call on the employee to work a further 48 hours per week was controlled and regulated by the content of the implied duty. However, one should be clear that this is not the same as saying that the implied duty cuts down or ousts the express term. Instead, as Lord Browne-Wilkinson explained, the scope of the employer's implied duty requires to be carved with reference to the express terms of the contract so that they can co-exist: that is to say the express term will fashion and influence the normative content of the implied duty and the standard of care, but will not supersede it.

In Chapter 3, we will examine the implied duties of the employee. Employees are also under an implied duty to exercise skill and care in the performance of their contractual duties.

The requisite standard of care

As Figure 2.2 demonstrates, whether the employer has breached the implied duty to exercise reasonable care depends on whether it took the requisite steps necessary to satisfy the standard of care. The standard of care and the nature and content of those steps will depend on the context and the circumstances of the case. If the standard of care is met by the employer, the court will hold that it has not breached the implied duty. If the employer has failed to meet the requisite standard, the court will hold that the employer has breached the implied duty. For some examples of breaches of duty, see Figure 2.4.

Examples of breach

Figure 2.4

Case name	Breach
Pagano [1976] IRLR 9	Unsafe vehicles
British Aircraft Corporation [1978] IRLR 332	Failure to provide eye protection
Graham Oxley, Tool Steels [1980] IRLR 135	Exposure to freezing working conditions
Waters [2000] IRLR 720	Failure to deal with complaint of sexual assault
Waltons and Morse [1997] IRLR 488	Failure to deal with smoky working environment

Psychiatric injury

In *Walker* v *Northumberland County Council* (1995), it was settled that the employer's implied duty to exercise reasonable care extends to the psychiatric well-being of the employee. A claimant employee must show that he is suffering from a recognised psychiatric illness which is attributable to the workplace. In *Sutherland* v *Hatton* (2002), the Court of Appeal outlined 16 practical propositions which govern:

- whether the employer has breached the implied duty;
- the issue of causation in the context of psychiatric harm.

You should familiarise yourself with these 16 propositions. In *Barber* v *Somerset County Council* (2004), the House of Lords approved these 16 guidelines as useful rules of thumb, but stated that they should not be treated as the equivalent of a statute. In *Hartman* v *South Essex Mental Health and Community Care NHS Trust* (2005), the Court of Appeal gave judgment in six appealed cases by applying the guidance in *Sutherland*.

✎ EXAM TIP

In problem questions, look out for any suggestion of an employee suffering from depression, anxiety or stress. Here, you should be thinking about the employer's implied duty to exercise reasonable care for the psychiatric well-being of the employee in the question. You should apply the guidelines in *Sutherland*, remembering that the employee must be suffering from a recognised psychiatric illness which is attributable to the workplace if the claim is to be successful.

▮ Duty to exercise reasonable care for the employee's economic and financial well-being?

An employer is under no implied duty to exercise reasonable care for the economic and financial well-being of its employees. Where:

- a particular term of the contract of employment makes available a valuable right to the employee;
- that right is contingent upon the employee taking action to avail himself of its benefit;
- the employee could not, in all the circumstances, reasonably be expected to be aware of the term unless it was drawn to his attention;
- there is no general implied duty on the part of the employer to take reasonable steps to bring it to the attention of the employee.

Such an implied duty may be owed, but this will depend on the facts and circumstances of the case and will not be implied as a matter of law into every contract of employment. This point was settled in *Crossley* v *Faithful & Gould Holdings Ltd* (2004), despite earlier indications to the contrary in the House of Lords in *Spring* v *Guardian Assurance plc* (1995) and *Scally* v *Southern Health and Social Services Board* (1992). However, there is an exception which was dealt with in *Spring*. Here it was held that an employer is under an implied duty to exercise reasonable care and skill in producing a reference.

■ Duty to cooperate?

An employee is under a duty to cooperate with his or her employer (see Chapter 3). It was always thought that this duty was not reciprocal. However, the case of *Takacs* v *Barclays Services Jersey Ltd* (2006) suggests otherwise. In *Takacs*, Master Fontaine in the High Court held that an employee had a prospect of succeeding in his claim that there was an implied term in his contract of employment that his employers would cooperate with him in fulfilling the condition for payment of the additional awards attached to a contractually guaranteed bonus. Whether this duty to cooperate will be recognised by higher authority is difficult to answer at this stage.

■ Duty to maintain and preserve trust and confidence

An employer owes a duty to its employees to maintain and preserve the trust and confidence inherent within the employment relationship. This implied term is mutual – it imposes an **implied duty of trust and confidence** on an employer and an implied duty of trust and confidence on an employee. The implied duty confers rights on the party to whom the implied duty is owed.

> **KEY DEFINITION: Implied term of mutual trust and confidence**
>
> A term of the contract of employment that each party will not, without reasonable and proper cause, act in such a way as would be calculated or likely to destroy or seriously damage the relationship of trust and confidence existing between it and the other party to the contract.

> **KEY CASE**
>
> *Malik* v *BCCI SA (in liquidation)* [1997] IRLR 462
>
> *Concerning: implied duty of mutual trust and confidence, example of breach*
>
> **Facts**
>
> A number of employees raised claims against their employer on the basis that the employer had breached an implied duty to maintain and preserve the trust and confidence inherent within the employment relationship by running a corrupt business. It was alleged that this implied duty existed as a matter of law. The employees were unable to secure alternative employment because of the stigma associated with having worked for BCCI. ▶

> **Legal principle**
>
> The House of Lords held that there was an implied term of the contract of employment that trust and confidence inherent in the employment relationship should be maintained and preserved. Translated into the language of implied duties, this imposes reciprocal duties on the employer and the employee to maintain such trust and confidence.

Controlling dismissal and suspension

In the cases of *Johnson* v *Unisys Ltd* (2001) and *Eastwood* v *Magnox Electric plc* (2004), the House of Lords held that the implied term could not be used to control or regulate the exercise of an employer's discretionary power to dismiss an employee. However, in *Gogay* v *Hertfordshire CC* (2000) the Court of Appeal held that the implied term could be breached where an employer exercised its power to suspend an employee.

KEY CASE

> *Johnson* v *Unisys Ltd* **[2001] IRLR 279**
>
> *Concerning: implied duty of mutual trust and confidence, dismissal*
>
> **Facts**
>
> An employee was successful in his unfair dismissal claim against an employer in the employment tribunal. He was awarded the maximum compensation allowable under statute at that time. Two years later, he raised an action in court for damages. He claimed that he had been wrongfully dismissed by the employer in breach of the employer's implied duty of trust and confidence.
>
> **Legal principle**
>
> The House of Lords held that an employee will not be awarded damages on the basis of wrongful dismissal where it was claimed that the act or manner of the dismissal breached the employer's implied duty of trust and confidence.

✎ EXAM TIP

In problem questions or essay questions, you should take care where the question involves an employee seeking to raise a claim for breach of the implied duty on the basis of the employer's act of dismissal or the manner of their dismissal. The law is clear in such situations to the effect that the implied duty will not be available to the employee to control that dismissal.

📖 REVISION NOTE

A breach of the implied term of mutual trust and confidence is the most common form of repudiatory breach of contract on the part of the employer which gives rise to a claim of wrongful dismissal or constructive dismissal for the purposes of the statutory unfair dismissal regime in Part X of the Employment Rights Act 1996 (ERA 1996). The law of wrongful dismissal is covered in Chapter 8. *Malik* v *BCCI SA*, *Johnson* v *Unisys Ltd* and *Eastwood* v *Magnox Electric plc* have implications for the claims that may be raised by an employee under the umbrella of a wrongful dismissal action in a court.

📖 REVISION NOTE

The law of **constructive dismissal** is covered in Chapter 9. It is absolutely essential that you understand that the implied term of mutual trust and confidence – and whether this term has been breached – lies at the heart of many constructive dismissal claims for the purposes of the statutory unfair dismissal regime in Part X of the ERA 1996 (see Chapter 9). In *Western Excavating (ECC) Ltd* v *Sharp* (1978) the Court of Appeal held that whether an employee had been constructively dismissed depended on whether the employer's conduct constituted a significant or repudiatory breach of contract going to the root of the contract of employment. Where the implied term of mutual trust and confidence is breached, this automatically amounts to a repudiatory breach – see *Morrow* v *Safeway Stores plc* (2002).

Abuse of discretion or power

The implied duty is principally used by an employee where an employer has exercised its express or implicit discretion, power, option or right in a way which is capricious, arbitrary or represents an abuse. For an analysis of key cases, see Figure 2.5.

Figure 2.5

Case name	Legal principle
BG plc [2001] IRLR 496	Implied term not concerned with the reasonableness of the employer's conduct
Croft [2002] IRLR 851	The implied duty can be used to call omissions to account
Hagen [2002] IRLR 31	Single acts of negligence will not usually amount to a breach
Transco plc (formerly BG plc) [2002] IRLR 444	Implied duty concerned with the control of arbitrary or capricious use of discretionary powers
Omilaju [2005] IRLR 35	Implied duty is available to strike down a course of conduct
French [1998] IRLR 646	The employer's decision to remove or vary an employee's terms and conditions of employment is subject to review
Greenhof [2006] IRLR 98	A breach of an employer's statutory duty to make reasonable adjustments in ss. 20–22 of the Equality Act 2010 was a breach

✎ **EXAM TIP**

In answering essay questions, you should bear in mind the key idea that the implied duty of trust and confidence operates in a way to regulate the abuse or arbitrary use of power or discretion by an employer. In addition, the implied duty may be breached where the employer engages in a course of conduct, or a series of actions or omissions, which cumulatively amount to a breach of duty. In answering problem questions, you should look out for employers' decisions which look like an abuse or arbitrary use of power (e.g. the removal of a bonus without consultation, the variation of key contractual terms or benefits without prior consultation, etc.).

✓ Make your answer stand out

The implied duty of trust and confidence is currently in an embryonic state. It continues to be developed piecemeal by the courts and tribunals on a case-by-case basis. The route of the implied term of mutual trust and confidence continues to ebb and flow and its final destination is yet to be located. An excellent student might consider two articles by Brodie (1998, 2001a), which are extremely valuable reading and could be employed in an exam situation to make an answer stand out.

■ Putting it all together

Answer guidelines

See the problem question at the start of this chapter. A diagram illustrating how to structure your answer is available on the website.

Approaching the question

There are four elements to this question and it is critical that you deal with each in turn in your answer. See below for further details.

Important points to include

Points to remember when answering this question:

■ In your introduction, make the point that Jonathan has a number of heads of claim open to him.

▶

- You should consider whether Jonathan has a claim on the basis that his employer has breached its implied duty to provide work – this will depend on the nature of his occupation.
- Consider the nature of Jonathan's claim in respect of the shares he is entitled to under his contract of employment. Is this right based on an implied term or an express term of the contract of employment?
- Jonathan's employer is in breach of its implied duty to exercise reasonable care for his physical well-being.

 Make your answer stand out

Consider whether there is scope for arguing that the implied term of mutual trust and confidence has been breached as a result of the actions of Jonathan's employer.

READ TO IMPRESS

Barmes, L. (2007) Common law implied terms and behavioural standards at work. 36 *Industrial Law Journal*: 35.

Brodie, D. (1996) The heart of the matter: mutual trust and confidence. 25 *Industrial Law Journal*: 121.

Brodie, D. (1998) Beyond exchange: the new contract of employment. 27 *Industrial Law Journal*: 79.

Brodie, D. (2001a) Legal coherence and the employment revolution. 117 *Law Quarterly Review*: 604.

Brodie, D. (2001b) Mutual trust and the values of the employment contract. 30 *Industrial Law Journal*: 84.

Brodie, D. (2008) Mutual trust and confidence: catalysts, constraints and commonality. 37 *Industrial Law Journal*: 329.

Cabrelli, D. (2005) The implied duty of mutual trust and confidence: an emerging overarching principle? 34 *Industrial Law Journal*: 284.

Van Bever, A. (2013) An employer's duty to provide information and advice on economic risks? 42 *Industrial Law Journal*: 1.

www.pearsoned.co.uk/lawexpress

 Go online to access more revision support including quizzes to test your knowledge, sample questions with answer guidelines, podcasts you can download, and more!

Implied terms of the contract of employment (2): duties of the employee

3

Revision checklist

Essential points you should know:

☐ The different types of implied duties owed by an employee

☐ The sources of the employee's implied duties

☐ The circumstances in which employees will be in breach of their duty to comply with the reasonable and lawful instructions of the employer

☐ The content, nature and scope of the employee's duty of fidelity and loyalty and the nature of the sub-duties which comprise the duty of fidelity and loyalty

■ Topic map

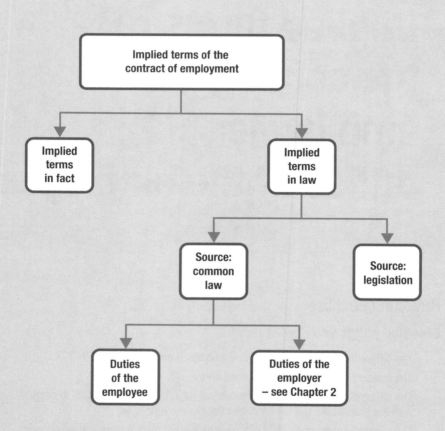

A printable version of this topic map is available from www.pearsoned.co.uk/lawexpress

■ Introduction

By operation of law, an employee owes a number of diverse implied duties to an employer.

This chapter concentrates on the implied terms of the contract of employment. In Chapter 2 we considered the implied duties of the employer and in this chapter we will concentrate on the employee's implied duties.

The implied duties arise by operation of law by virtue of the fact that the employer and employee have entered into a contract of employment. The implied duties have (i) the common law and (ii) legislation as their source. In this chapter, we will consider the implied duties having the common law as their source only. We will also examine how these common law based implied duties have been influenced by legislation.

ASSESSMENT ADVICE

Essay questions

These require broad general knowledge of the implied duties of the employee. In particular, the examiner will be looking for an examination of the development of the implied duties and whether the current position is satisfactory. The examiner may also expect you to address the sources, content, nature and scope of application of the implied duties. Since the implied duties are based on the common law, an understanding of key cases in respect of each of the implied duties will be expected. In tackling essay questions, you should always directly answer the question(s) asked and apply the relevant law.

Problem questions

Generally, problem questions involve an examination of more than one of the implied duties of the employee. This may also be combined with other areas of employment law, for example:

■ the implied duties of the employer;

■ the statutory duties of the employer or the employee; and/or

■ the effect of the express terms of the contract of employment on the implied duties of the employee.

Problem questions concentrating on the implied duties of an employee may be framed in such a way that you are asked to advise the employee whether there is a reasonable prospect of success in raising a claim in an employment tribunal, or a legal action in the courts. In tackling problem questions, you should always directly answer the question(s) asked and apply the relevant law to the facts at hand.

■ Sample question

Could you answer this question? Below is a typical essay question that could arise on this topic. Guidelines on answering the question are included at the end of the chapter, while a sample problem question and guidance on tackling it can be found on the companion website.

ESSAY QUESTION

Critically evaluate the content and scope of the employee's implied duty of fidelity and loyalty.

■ Duty to obey reasonable and lawful instructions and orders

An employee is under a duty to comply with the reasonable and lawful instructions of his employer. However, the employee is excused from performance where the employer's instructions or orders are unreasonable or unlawful. There is also an exception to the general rule: an employee is not bound to follow the reasonable instructions or orders of the employer where this will expose the employee and others to unjustifiable risks.

KEY CASE

Pepper v Webb **[1969] 1 WLR 514**

Concerning: implied duty to comply with reasonable and lawful instructions or orders of employer

Facts

Webb's wife appointed Mr Pepper as head gardener. An incident occurred after Webb's wife instructed Pepper to plant some plants. Pepper refused. Webb subsequently asked Pepper to plant the plants. Pepper again refused in strong terms. Thereupon, Webb summarily dismissed Pepper.

Legal principle

Webb and his wife's instructions were reasonable and lawful. Hence, Pepper was in repudiatory breach of contract in failing to comply with such instructions. Contrast the facts of this case and outcome with *Wilson v Racher* (1974).

KEY CASE

Donovan v *Invicta Airways Ltd* [1970] 1 Lloyd's Rep 486

Concerning: exception, implied duty to comply with reasonable and lawful instructions or orders of employer

Facts

Donovan was a freelance air pilot. On a number of occasions, for the purposes of speed or economy, his employer:

(1)   invited him to fly contrary to regulations;

(2)   failed to maintain the aircraft in a safe condition; and

(3)   was discourteous to him.

Legal principle

The employer's instructions to fly the aircraft in such circumstances exposed the employee and others (e.g. passengers and the public) to unjustifiable risks. Accordingly, the employee had not breached his implied duty to comply with reasonable and lawful instructions or orders of the employer. Instead, the employer's conduct was such that it amounted to a repudiatory breach of the contract of employment.

Limitations on implied duty to obey reasonable and lawful instructions and orders

Students often fail to appreciate that the implied duty of the employee is subject to the statutory employment rights of employees. For example, employees will not be in breach of the implied duty if they refuse an employer's instruction to perform a particular task on the basis that they are exercising their right to take a reasonable amount of time off from work to deal with a crisis relating to their dependants in terms of section 57A of the Employment Rights Act 1996 (ERA 1996). Likewise, there is no breach of duty where an employee refuses an employer's instructions to work in excess of 48 hours in breach of regulation 4(1) of the Working Time Regulations 1998.

✎ EXAM TIP

In a problem question, look out for any suggestion that an employee is being asked to comply with an instruction or order. You should then consider whether the instruction:

■ is unlawful or unreasonable;

■ exposes the employee to unjustifiable or unquantifiable risks; or

■ is incompatible with an employee's statutory rights.

If so, the employee will be excused from performance.

■ Duty to indemnify employer

An employee is under an obligation to indemnify his employer where his actions result in loss to the employer.

■ Duty to exercise care and perform duties competently

An employee is under a duty to exercise the normal degree of skill and care in the performance of his work. An employee must also perform his duties in a competent manner. An employee should not follow the reasonable and lawful instructions or orders of the employer in a literal fashion which has the effect of disrupting the business of the employer, e.g. a 'work to rule' policy.

KEY CASE

Lister v *Romford Ice and Cold Storage* Co. *Ltd* [1957] AC 555

Concerning: implied duty to exercise care, breach

Facts

A lorry driver employee negligently drove his lorry, injuring his father who was a fellow employee. The employer was held to be vicariously liable for the actions of the lorry driver and so the father recovered damages from the employer. The employer then sued the lorry driver on the basis that the latter had breached this implied duty.

Legal principle

The employee had been in breach of duty. Hence, his employer was entitled to recover damages from him in the amount for which they had been made liable to his father.

！ Don't be tempted to . . .

Be careful not to fall into the trap of thinking that an employee injured by a colleague can only sue that colleague. Indeed, where an employee causes an injury to a fellow employee, the injured employee can seek redress from the employer. This is based on the tortious or delictual (in Scotland) doctrine of vicarious liability, whereby the employer assumes liability for the negligent actions of the employee in the scope of the employee's employment. Thereafter, as occurred in *Lister*, an employer who has been held vicariously liable may seek indemnification from the negligent employee in respect of the losses which it sustains in paying out compensation to the injured employee. Whether the employer adopts such a course of action is essentially a matter for its insurers.

KEY CASE

Secretary of State for Employment v *Associated Society of Locomotive Engineers and Firemen* [1972] 2 QB 443 and 455

Concerning: breach of implied duty to perform duties competently

Facts

Pursuant to an industrial dispute, three trade unions instructed their member employees to work strictly in accordance with their employer's rule book, i.e. 'work to rule' as a means of disrupting the employer's business.

Legal principle

The Court of Appeal held that the employees were breaching their contract of employment. It was held that each employee would not, in obeying lawful instructions, seek to carry them out in a manner which had the effect of disrupting the employer's business.

✎ EXAM TIP

In an essay question or problem question, look out for any assertion in the question that the employees are complying with the strict letter of the employer's handbook or rule book, i.e. 'work to rule'. Where an employee does so, this will commonly have a negative effect on the business of the employer in lost time and revenues. In each case, this will be a matter of fact and degree and you will be required to offer a reasoned view on this point.

■ Duty to adapt and cooperate

Over time, an employer may restructure the methods of the workplace or the manner in which an employee is expected to perform his duties. Where these changes are adopted, an employee is expected to adapt and cooperate with the employer in the introduction of such changes. Employees will be in breach of duty if they fail to do so.

KEY CASE

Cresswell v *Board of Inland Revenue* [1984] IRLR 190

Concerning: implied duty to adapt and cooperate with employer

Facts

The employer introduced a new computer system for the purposes of simplifying and rendering more efficient the method by which PAYE was calculated, administered and paid. A crisis ensued when the employees refused to use the new computer system and the employer withdrew permission from the employees to use the old system, refusing to pay them while they rejected it. ▶

> **Legal principle**
>
> The employees were in breach of contract. An employee is under an obligation to adapt to new working methods and cooperate with the employer in introducing such systems or techniques.

Content and nature of the implied duty

It was recognised in *Cresswell* that it will be difficult to assess when a new working method, pattern or technique is so pronounced that it in fact represents a new job which the employee is being asked to perform. Where the changes are so great that the job description has effectively changed, the change will amount to an attempt by the employer unilaterally to vary the terms of the employee's contract of employment. In such circumstances, employees will be relieved from their duty to adapt and cooperate. In *Cresswell*, it was held that it was a question of fact whether the introduction of new methods and techniques altered the nature of the work to such a degree that it was no longer the work that the employee had agreed to perform under the terms of his contract.

■ Duty to maintain and preserve trust and confidence

The duty to maintain and preserve the trust and confidence inherent in the employment relationship is mutual. In this chapter, we consider the implied duty imposed on an employee which confers rights on an employer. Since the implied duty is mutual, its content, scope, nature and source is the same in any given case, regardless of whether it is the employer or employee who it is alleged owes or has breached the duty.

KEY CASE

Briscoe v *Lubrizol Ltd* [2002] IRLR 607

Concerning: implied duty to maintain trust and confidence, breach

Facts

An employee on long-term sick leave was being paid sums by insurers via his employer, in terms of a disability payment insurance scheme. The insurers subsequently rejected the employer's right to claim on behalf of the employee under the scheme. The employer corresponded, and arranged meetings, with the employee to discuss matters, which the employee ignored.

> **Legal principle**
>
> The employee had been in repudiatory breach in wilfully failing to respond to the employer's correspondence and attend meetings. Such actions on the part of an employee undermined the trust and confidence inherent in the contract of employment and so the employee was in breach of duty.

■ Duty of fidelity, loyalty and confidentiality

An employee is under an implied duty of fidelity and loyalty to his or her employer. Whether such a duty has been breached in a particular case will depend on the facts and circumstances. The effect of a breach by an employee is that an employer is entitled to sue for damages.

Content and nature of the implied duty

The implied duty of fidelity, loyalty and confidentiality of the employee can be divided into six sub-duties. There is some overlap between each of them (see Figure 3.1).

Figure 3.1

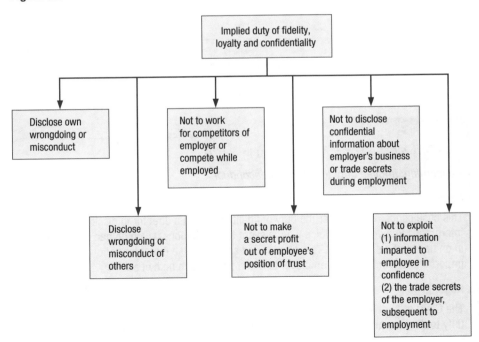

Duty to disclose own wrongdoing

The cases of *Bell* v *Lever Brothers Ltd* (1932) and *Sybron Corp.* v *Rochem Ltd* (1983) established that an employee is not under an obligation to disclose his own wrongdoing or misdeeds to his employer. However, in the case of *Item Software (UK) Ltd* v *Fassihi* (2004), the Court of Appeal held that a senior employee who was also a director does owe such a duty to his or her employer. For a summary of the legal developments in this area, see Figure 3.2.

Figure 3.2

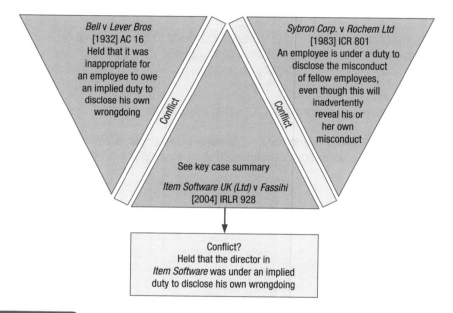

Item Software (UK) Ltd v *Fassihi* **[2004] IRLR 928**

Concerning: implied duty to disclose misconduct

Facts

This case concerned whether the duty of fidelity required a director to disclose important information known to him which was relevant to negotiations which he had been involved in on behalf of his employer. The director had sought to use that information to divert an important contract from his employer to a company which he owned.

Legal principle

The Court of Appeal held that as a matter of policy, a director, being a fiduciary, is under a duty to disclose his own wrongdoing or misconduct to his or her employer.

✎ EXAM TIP

In an essay or problem question, do not put forward the proposition that employees are not obliged to disclose their own misconduct. The extent to which the duty to disclose wrongdoing applies to employees in general is not wholly clear from the judgments of the Court of Appeal in *Item Software (UK) Ltd* v *Fassihi* (2004). If the employee *is not a fiduciary, Ranson* v *Customer Systems plc* (2012) is an authority for the proposition that an employee may be subject to a duty to disclose his own wrongdoing and that whether such a duty is implied is dependent on the terms of his employment contract. Therefore, what does appear clear is that:

- *Bell* v *Lever Brothers Ltd* (1932) is not an authority for the proposition that there are no circumstances in which an employee can have a duty to disclose his own wrongdoing;
- employees who engage in illegal or fraudulent activities will be under such a duty to disclose, provided that they are acting as a fiduciary of the employer or where the employer has expressly imparted trust and confidence in them.

See Berg (2005) for further reading.

Duty to disclose wrongdoing or misconduct of other employees or colleagues

Where employees become aware of the misconduct or wrongdoing of other employees, they are under a duty to disclose such misconduct to their employer. See *Sybron Corp.* v *Rochem Ltd* (1983) and *Shepherds Investments Ltd* v *Andrew Walters* (2007), but compare this with the approach of Mr Justice Hickinbottom in the High Court in *Lonmar Global Risks Ltd (formerly SBJ Global Risks Ltd)* v *West* (2011).

Duty not to work for competitors of the employer or compete with employer

Employees owe an implied obligation not to:

- work for enterprises which compete with their employer; or
- trade directly in competition with their employer.

The competing activities may take place during their own spare time or the working time of their employer.

KEY CASE

Hivac v Park Royal Scientific Instruments **[1946] Ch 169**

Concerning: implied duty not to work for competitors, breach

Facts

The employer manufactured valves. Its employees were extremely skilled in assembling those valves. On Sundays during their day off, the employees assembled valves for competitors of their employer.

Legal principle

The Court of Appeal held that the employees had breached the duty of good faith and fidelity, despite the fact that the work undertaken for the competitor was conducted in their own spare time.

! Don't be tempted to . . .

You may be asked in an essay or problem question to provide advice as to whether an employee is competing with his/her employer. Don't fall into the trap of thinking that employees are entitled to compete with the employer in their own spare time. Where an employee intends to leave the employment of the employer for the purposes of setting up in competition with his employer and before or after so leaving does not disclose or exploit the confidential information or trade secrets of the employer, it is a matter of fact and degree whether an employee:

1. is actually competing with his employer; or

2. simply has the intention of setting up in competition with the employer in the future.

Situation 1 amounts to a breach of duty, whereas situation 2 does not. Which side of the divide between 1 and 2 the actions of the employee will fall is a matter of fact and degree (see Figure 3.3).

! Don't be tempted to . . .

An essay or problem question may ask you whether employees are entitled to compete with their employers once they cease to be employed. You should avoid the pitfall of saying that employees will invariably in all circumstances have the right to compete with their employers post-employment. Whilst an employee is free to compete with his employer subsequent to the termination of his contract of employment, an express term called a restrictive covenant may be included in his contract of employment which prohibits him from competing with a competitor of his employer or setting up in competition with his employer after employment. The common law position is that such a 'non-compete' restrictive covenant is contrary to public policy and will be enforceable only so long as it is no wider than necessary to provide reasonable and adequate protection of the legitimate interests of the employer.

Figure 3.3

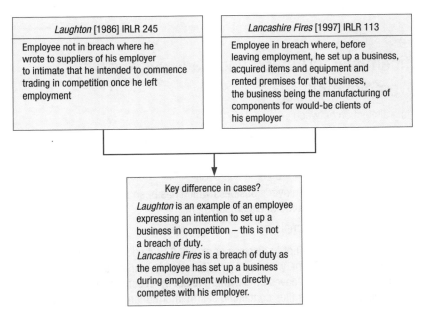

Duty not to make a secret profit

An employee is under an implied duty not to make a secret profit out of his or her position without the knowledge or consent of the employer. Where such a secret profit has been generated, the employee must account to the employer for it.

Confidential information and trade secrets: during employment

During the course of their employment, employees are under an implied duty not to disclose or exploit confidential information about their employer's business or the trade secrets of their employer. An employer can seek an injunction or interdict to restrain the employee from making disclosure. However, during the course of their employment, employees are entitled to disclose or exploit the general skill and knowledge which they have amassed during that period.

✎ **EXAM TIP**

An employee's obligation not to disclose or exploit confidential information about the employer's business or the trade secrets of the employer is not absolute. Sections 43A–43L of the ERA 1996 offer protections to employees who release confidential information in relation to their employer's business to various parties where such disclosure is in the public interest. Furthermore, the implied duty not to disclose confidential information is subject to the employee's right to freedom of expression in Article 10 of the European Convention on Human Rights (incorporated into UK law by virtue of Schedule 1 to the Human Rights Act 1998).

Confidential information and trade secrets: after employment

There is a distinction between:

1. the general skill, know-how and knowledge which an employee has;
2. information about the employer's business which is in the public domain or has been learnt by the employee during the course of his employment;
3. information about the employer's business which has been imparted to the employee in confidence during the course of his employment;
4. the trade secrets of the employer.

An employee is under a duty not to disclose or exploit 3 or 4 subsequent to the date of termination of his employment, whereas 1 and 2 are freely transferable. A clear example of 4 arises where an employee leaves employment to set up in competition with the employer and before doing so transfers files containing secret information to a USB key, taking it away with him and subsequently exploiting it.

KEY CASE

Faccenda Chicken Ltd v Fowler **[1986] IRLR 69**

Concerning: implied duty not to disclose trade secrets subsequent to date of termination of employment

Facts

The employer's business was the sale of fresh chickens. The employee was the sales manager. Thus, he was privy to customer lists, pricing policies and information regarding the quantity and quality of the goods sold. The employee left employment to set up in competition with his employer, selling the same products to the same clients.

Legal principle

The information used by the employee was not information about the employer's business which had been imparted to the employee in confidence during the course of his employment. Nor did it amount to the trade secrets of the employer. Accordingly, the employee was not in breach of the implied duty of fidelity. See Figure 3.4.

Figure 3.4

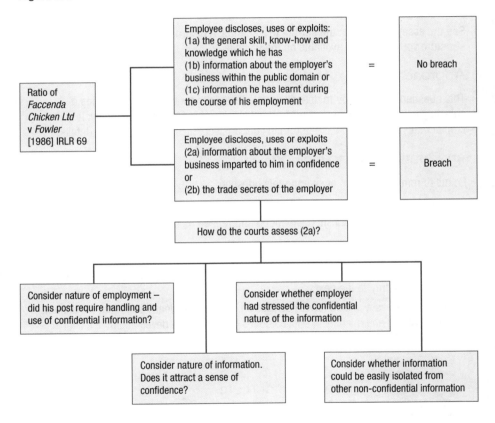

Restrictive covenants

It is open to an employer to include restrictive covenants in the contract of employment of the employee. These may restrict the employee from disclosing *any* confidential information or trade secrets of the employer subsequent to employment. Such express terms complement the implied terms of the contract of employment, thus increasing the protection available to the employer. The common law position is that such restrictive covenants are contrary to public policy and will be enforceable only so long as they are no wider than necessary to provide reasonable and adequate protection of the legitimate interests of the employer.

■ Putting it all together

Answer guidelines

See the essay question at the start of this chapter. A diagram illustrating how to structure your answer is available on the website.

Approaching the question

This question requires you to describe and analyse the six separate categories of sub-duty which together comprise the employee's duty of loyalty and fidelity. It is crucial that you deal with each in turn in your answer. See below for further details.

Important points to include

Points to remember when answering this question:

- Refer to the implied duties having the common law as their source. The implied duties have been established, amended and refined by the courts over time on a case-by-case basis.

- Take each implied duty in turn and analyse and explain its content, nature and scope in a methodical manner. There should be a clear structure and a logical flow from one implied duty to the next.

- Finally, your essay should have a conclusion. This should clearly state that the content, scope, nature and quantity of implied duties continue to be developed by the courts and tribunals in light of statutory, social, economic and political developments.

 Make your answer stand out

- Address the possible path and future development of the implied duties.

- Include a brief discussion of the extent to which statutory developments and express contractual provisions have affected or may affect the implied duties.

- Comment on the common law source of the implied duties and the extent to which this renders it unlikely that the list of implied duties could ever be closed.

READ TO IMPRESS

Berg, A. (2005) Fiduciary duties: a director's duty to disclose his own misconduct. 121 *Law Quarterly Review*. 213.

Clark, L. (1999) Mutual trust and confidence, fiduciary relationships and duty of disclosure. 30 *Industrial Law Journal*. 348.

Flannigan, R. (2008) The fiduciary duty of fidelity. 124 *Law Quarterly Review*. 274.

Simms, V. (2001) Is employment a fiduciary relationship? 30 *Industrial Law Journal*. 101.

www.pearsoned.co.uk/lawexpress

 Go online to access more revision support including quizzes to test your knowledge, sample questions with answer guidelines, podcasts you can download, and more!

Key statutory employment rights

4

Revision checklist

Essential points you should know:

- [ ] The key statutory rights of employees and workers under the Employment Rights Act 1996 and the Employment Relations Act 1999

- [ ] The rights of workers under the National Minimum Wage Act 1998

- [ ] Maternity, paternity and parental leave rights in terms of the Employment Rights Act 1996, the Maternity and Parental Leave etc. Regulations 1999, the Shared Parental Leave Regulations 2014 and the Paternity and Adoption Leave Regulations 2002

- [ ] The rights of employees under subordinate legislation such as the Working Time Regulations 1998, the Part-Time Workers (Prevention of Less Favourable Treatment) Regulations 2000 and the Fixed-Term Employees (Prevention of Less Favourable Treatment) Regulations 2002

■ Topic map

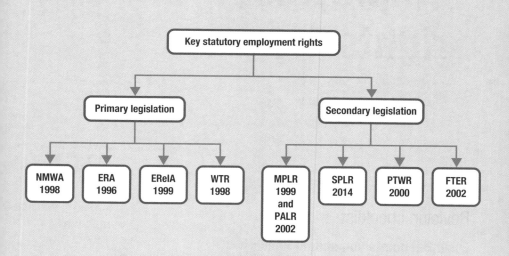

■ Introduction

Employment protection legislation confers a number of statutory rights upon employees.

This chapter concentrates on a selection of the statutory rights of employees. The sources of these rights vary from primary legislation, such as the Employment Rights Act 1996 and the National Minimum Wage Act 1998, to secondary legislation, such as the Working Time Regulations 1998 and the Part-Time Workers (Prevention of Less Favourable Treatment) Regulations 2000. In recent years, a high proportion of secondary legislation conferring statutory employment rights has originated from the European Union.

ASSESSMENT ADVICE

Essay questions

These require broad general knowledge of the main statutory rights of the employee. The examiner will also be looking for an examination of the main stimuli for the creation of some of the statutory rights, namely the EU. In addressing the broader aspects of the key statutory employment rights, the examiner will also expect you to address the proper method of enforcement of such statutory rights. In tackling essay questions, you should always directly answer the question(s) asked and apply the relevant law.

Problem questions

Where a problem question requires you to address key statutory employment rights, you will be required to demonstrate that you have identified and interpreted the relevant primary or secondary legislation in the correct manner. Moreover, you will be expected to take into account any potential exceptions and the appropriate means of enforcement of these rights. If the source of a statutory employment right is EU law, the implications of this should also be considered. On this point, see Chapter 1. In tackling problem questions, you should always directly answer the question(s) asked and apply the relevant law to the facts at hand.

■ Sample question

Could you answer this question? Below is a typical problem question that could arise on this topic. Guidelines on answering the question are included at the end of the chapter, while a sample essay question and guidance on tackling it can be found on the companion website.

Rights under the National Minimum Wage Act 1998

The National Minimum Wage Act 1998 (NMWA 1998) contains two key protections in the context of the minimum wage. The NMWA 1998 is complemented by the National Minimum Wage Regulations 2015 (the NMW Regs) and the national minimum wage is set by the Secretary of State annually by regulations. The National Minimum Wage has been relabelled as the National Living Wage and set at £7.20 per hour for those aged 25 or over since April 2016.

KEY STATUTE

NMWA 1998, s. 1(1)

A person who qualifies for the national minimum wage shall be remunerated by his employer in respect of his work in any pay reference period at a rate which is not less than the national minimum wage.

KEY STATUTE

NMWA 1998, s. 23(1)

A worker has the right not to be subjected to any detriment by any act, or any deliberate failure to act, by his employer, done on the ground that –

(a) any action was taken, or was proposed to be taken, by or on behalf of the worker with a view to enforcing, or otherwise securing the benefit of, a right of the worker's. . .; or. . .

(b) the worker qualifies, or will or might qualify, for the national minimum wage or for a particular rate of national minimum wage.

Enforcement of NMWA 1998, ss. 1 and 23

Section 17 of the NMWA 1998 demonstrates that an employee's right under section 1 of the NMWA 1998 is enforceable by raising an action for a breach of the terms of his contract of employment in the courts or by presenting a complaint to an employment tribunal. Hence, although a statutory provision, section 1 confers a contractual right upon an employee. Meanwhile, the appropriate method of enforcement of section 23 of the NMWA 1998 is the presentation of a complaint to an employment tribunal in terms of section 24.

KEY CASE

Leisure Employment Services Ltd v Commissioners for HM Revenue & Customs **[2007] IRLR 450**

Concerning: employer's costs and expenses falling within the 'living accommodation' offset

Facts

Where employers provide accommodation to their workers, the NMW Regs entitle employers to deduct 'living accommodation' expenses from the workers' pay, subject to a stipulated maximum (which is changed annually) for each day. Thus, accommodation is the only benefit in kind which may be taken into account towards national minimum wage pay. Here, the employer of workers living in on-site chalets and caravans at Butlins made the maximum 'living accommodation' offset, but also deducted expenses for heat and light from workers' pay on a fortnightly basis. The effect was that the workers received less than the national minimum wage. HM Revenue and Customs brought enforcement proceedings against the employer.

Legal principle

The Court of Appeal held that the charge for heat and light was required to be taken into account as part of the 'living accommodation' charge. Thus, since the sums charged were in excess of the maximum 'living accommodation' offset, the employer was in breach of the NMWA 1998 and the NMW Regs.

📖 REVISION NOTE

The statutory right of a worker to be paid the national minimum wage should be taken into account when considering the implied duty of the employer to pay the employee wages even where there is no work (see Chapter 2). Provided the employee is ready and willing to work, payment will be due by the employer at the minimum wage.

Rights under the Employment Rights Act 1996

The Employment Rights Act 1996 (ERA 1996) provides a large number of statutory rights to employees. This chapter seeks to outline only some of them and the means by which they are enforced.

The right to receive a statement of the particulars of employment

Employees have a statutory right to receive certain information about their employment under section 1(1) and (2) of ERA 1996. Sections 1(3), (4), (5), 2, 3 and 4 specify the 'particulars of employment' referred to in ERA 1996, section 1(1) and (2). Section 11 of the Act provides that the rights in ERA 1996, section 1(1) and (2) are to be enforced by presenting a complaint to an employment tribunal.

The right of an employee not to suffer unauthorised deductions from his wages

Subject to certain exceptions, the employer is prohibited from deducting sums from the wages of a worker.

ERA 1996, section 23(1) provides that the right in section 13(1) is to be enforced by presenting a complaint to an employment tribunal. 'Wages' are defined in section 27 ERA 1996. In *Delaney* v *Staples* (1992), it was held that a payment in lieu of notice to an employee where that employee had been summarily dismissed did not fall within the definition of 'wages' in section 27 ERA 1996. Instead, it was a payment in connection with the termination of the employee's employment.

KEY STATUTE

ERA 1996, s. 13(1)

An employer shall not make a deduction from wages of a worker employed by him unless –

(a) the deduction is required or authorised to be made by virtue of a statutory provision or a relevant provision of the worker's contract, or

(b) the worker has previously signified in writing his agreement or consent to the making of the deduction.

The right of an employee not to suffer any detriment

ERA 1996, sections 44, 45A, 47 and 47A–47E each provide that an employee is not to suffer any detriment at the hands of an employer for a number of reasons, including the following:

- a failure to obey the employer's orders for health and safety reasons;
- a refusal on the part of the employee to comply with a requirement imposed by the employer which is in contravention of the Working Time Regulations 1998;
- the making of a protected disclosure by the employee.

In terms of ERA 1996, section 48, each of the employee's rights under ERA 1996, sections 44, 45A, 47 and 47A–47E are to be enforced by presenting a complaint to an employment tribunal.

The right to receive minimum periods of notice

If an employer proposes to terminate the employment of an employee, statute dictates that certain minimum periods of notice must be given by the former to the latter.

KEY STATUTE

ERA 1996, s. 86(1)

The notice required to be given by an employer to terminate the contract of employment of a person who has been continuously employed for one month or more –

(a) is not less than one week's notice if his period of continuous employment is less than two years,

(b) is not less than one week's notice for each year of continuous employment if his period of continuous employment is two years or more but less than twelve years, and

(c) is not less than twelve weeks' notice if his period of continuous employment is twelve years or more.

Where an employer fails to observe the terms of ERA 1996, section 86(1), an employee is entitled to enforce this right by raising a court action for a breach of the terms of his contract of employment.

The right to be provided with a written statement of the reasons for dismissal

When an employee's employment is terminated by an employer with or without notice, the employer must provide the employee with a written statement of the reasons for his dismissal under ERA 1996, section 92(1). The right in section 92(1) is enforceable by presenting a complaint to an employment tribunal in terms of ERA 1996, section 93(1)(a).

Rights under the Employment Relations Act 1999

Section 10 of the Employment Relations Act 1999 (ERelA 1999) affords a key right to a worker. It enables a worker to be accompanied by a colleague or trade union employee or official at a disciplinary or grievance hearing. However, only in exceptional cases will a worker have the right to be accompanied by a legally qualified practitioner such as a solicitor: *R (on the application of G)* v *Governors of X School* (2011). The worker's companion has the right to address the hearing, put forward the worker's case, sum up the case and respond on the worker's behalf to any view expressed at the hearing. Under section 12 of the ERelA 1999, the worker has the right not to suffer any detriment or dismissal because he/she exercised such a right. The rights afforded to the worker under section 10 of the ERelA 1999 are enforceable by raising a complaint in an employment tribunal by virtue of section 11(1).

Rights under the Working Time Regulations 1998

Rights are conferred on workers in terms of the Working Time Regulations 1998 (WTR 1998). We will concentrate on the four principal rights conferred by the WTR 1998. The source of the rights in the WTR 1998 is EC Directive 2003/88/EC (OJ 2003 L299/9) of 4 November 2003 concerning certain aspects of the organisation of working time. For a summary of some domestic legislation, which is based on EU law, see Figure 4.1.

Figure 4.1

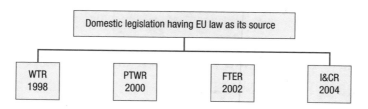

Maximum weekly working time

An employee has a statutory right not to be compelled to work in excess of an average of 48 hours in a working week.

KEY STATUTE

WTR 1998, reg. 4(1) and (2)

(1) Unless his employer has first obtained the worker's agreement in writing to perform such work a worker's time, including overtime, in any reference period which is applicable in his case shall not exceed an average of 48 hours for each seven days.

(2) An employer shall take all reasonable steps, in keeping with the need to protect the health and safety of workers, to ensure that the limit specified in Paragraph (1) is complied with in the case of each worker employed by him in relation to whom it applies. . .

Enforcement of WTR 1998, reg. 4(1) and (2)

The key mechanism for the enforcement of regulation 4(1) of the WTR 1998 was explained in the case of *Barber* v *RJB Mining (UK) Ltd* (1999). It confers a contractual right on an employee (and a corresponding contractual obligation on the employer) which is enforceable by a common law action. Meanwhile, a failure on the part of an employer to comply with regulation 4(2) of the WTR 1998 can be addressed by criminal sanction only. The right cannot be enforced by presenting a complaint to an employment tribunal. Moreover, *Sayers* v *Cambridgeshire County Council* (2007) decided that a breach of regulation 4(2) of the WTR 1998 does not give rise to a cause of action for breach of statutory duty.

WTR 1998 opt-out

The importance of the words 'Unless his employer has first obtained the worker's agreement in writing to perform such work' in regulation 4(1) of the WTR 1998 cannot be stressed enough. These words enable an employer to opt out of the 48-hour weekly limit. This is achieved by obtaining the employee's consent in a written agreement. See Barnard, Deakin and Hobbs (2003) for a discussion of the pervasiveness of opt-outs in the UK. At the time of writing, the European Commission has closed a consultation exercise with a view to amending the EC Working Time Directive 2003/88/EC of November 2003 to include provisions for the monitoring of employers' exercise of the opt-out. However, the historical records do not augur well for this initiative: earlier attempts to reach political agreement on the removal of the opt-out broke down in 2009 when the European Parliament and the Council of the European Union were unable to reach consensus.

'On-call' time

Regulation 2 of the WTR 1998 defines 'working time' as any period during which the employee is working, is at his employer's disposal and carrying out his activity or duties. On this basis, does time spent by an employee on call at or outside the workplace constitute working time?

KEY CASE

SIMAP v *Conselleria de Sanidad y Consumo de la Generalidad Valenciana* **[2000] IRLR 845**

Concerning: 'on-call' time, working time

Facts

A trade union for doctors in Spain (SIMAP) raised a claim against the Ministry of Health for the Valencia Region in Spain. They argued that 'working time' covered time spent on call by the doctors at a health centre.

Legal principle

The ECJ held that time spent on call by the doctors amounted to 'working time'. The key factor in this case was that the doctors were required to be present at a health centre when they were working on call. Hence, where a worker spends time on call, but is free to pursue his own leisure interests and does not require to be present or available at a particular workplace location, such time will not be included in determining 'working time'.

Daily rest and weekly rest

An employee has the right to daily rest and weekly rest breaks.

KEY STATUTE

WTR 1998, regs. 10(1) and 11(1)

10(1) A worker is entitled to a rest period of not less than eleven consecutive hours in each 24-hour period during which he works for his employer.

11(1) Subject to Paragraph (2), a worker is entitled to an uninterrupted rest period of not less than 24 hours in each seven-day period during which he works for his employer.

The rights afforded to the worker under the WTR 1998, regulations 10(1) and 11(1) can be enforced by raising a complaint in an employment tribunal by virtue of regulation 30(1)(a) of the WTR 1998.

Annual leave

Regulation 13(1) of the WTR 1998 provides an employee with the right to a minimum of 28 days' paid annual leave in a holiday year. It is enforceable by presenting a complaint to an employment tribunal.

KEY CASE

***Robinson-Steele* v *RD Retail Services Ltd* [2006] IRLR 386**

Concerning: 'rolled-up' holiday pay, annual leave

Facts

Workers claimed that their employer had not paid them the holiday pay to which they were entitled under regulation 13(1) of the WTR 1998. The workers had been paid 'rolled-up' holiday pay, i.e. although the workers received no pay when they took their holidays, they were given additional payment during the weeks that they worked.

Legal principle

The ECJ held that the payment of 'rolled-up' holiday pay was unlawful under the EC Working Time Directive 2003/88/EC of 4 November 2003.

Right not to suffer a detriment under ERA 1996, s. 45A

Section 45A of the ERA 1996 complements the WTR 1998. It provides that a worker has the right not to be subjected to any detriment by any act, or any deliberate failure to act, by his employer on certain grounds, e.g. that the worker:

- refused to comply with an employer's instruction which contravened the WTR 1998;
- refused to give up a right conferred by the WTR 1998; or
- brought proceedings against the employer to enforce a right under the WTR 1998.

A worker can enforce the right under section 45A of the ERA 1996 by presenting a complaint to an employment tribunal under section 48(1ZA) of the Act.

■ Maternity, paternity and parental leave rights

Maternity rights

Sections 71 and 73 of the ERA 1996 and regulations 4 and 7 of the Maternity and Parental Leave etc. Regulations 1999 (MPLR 1999) provide an employee with the right to:

- 26 weeks' ordinary maternity leave (OML);
- 26 weeks' additional maternity leave (AML) from work.

During the periods of OML and AML, the employee continues to have the benefit of her terms and conditions of employment, including non-pay benefits (such as company car, gym membership, contractual holidays and health insurance) with the exception of pay. The employee is entitled to the payment of statutory maternity pay for 39 weeks by virtue of the Statutory Maternity Pay (General) Regulations 1986 (SI 1986/1960), regulation 2(2) and the Social Security Contributions and Benefits Act 1992, sections 164–167. In terms of section 72 of the ERA 1996 and regulation 8 of the MPLR 1999, an employee has a right to compulsory maternity leave of two weeks, which commences with the day on which childbirth occurs. If an employee is subjected to a detriment by her employer for reasons connected with maternity leave, she may present a complaint to an employment tribunal under sections 47C and 48(1) of the ERA 1996.

Paternity rights

Provided an employee is able to satisfy:

- that he is the father of a child or married to or the civil partner or partner of a child's mother;
- the other conditions in terms of regulation 4(2) of the Paternity and Adoption Leave Regulations 2002 (PALR 2002),

he is entitled to be absent from work on paternity leave in terms of regulation 4(2) of the PALR 2002 for the purpose of caring for a child or supporting the child's mother. An employee may take:

- one week's paternity leave; or
- two consecutive weeks' leave unpaid.

Provided that the employee is able to satisfy particular conditions, he will also be entitled to take shared parental leave. This is a form of 'leave transfer' whereby a period of the mother's OML or AML is transferred to the father of the child or partner of the mother: the Shared Parental Leave Regulations (SI 2014/3050). The shared parental leave (SPL) regime enables eligible employees – rather than mothers or adopting parents – to share up to 52 weeks' leave as SPL and 39 weeks' shared statutory paternity pay (SSPP) on the birth or adoption of a child. The default position is that mothers will continue to be entitled to maternity leave and statutory maternity pay, but that mothers with partners who both meet certain qualifying conditions will be permitted to end the mother's maternity leave and statutory maternity pay and convert it into SPL and SSPP. Accordingly, the untaken balance of maternity leave and statutory maternity pay will then be available to both the mother and partner as SPL and SSPP and can be taken in blocks of one week. The untaken balance of maternity leave and statutory maternity pay may be shared in a manner which enables both parents to be on leave concurrently. However, the first two weeks after the child's birth are reserved to the mother as leave, and cannot be shared pursuant to SPL.

If an employee is subjected to a detriment by his employer for reasons connected with paternity leave, he may present a complaint to an employment tribunal under sections 47C and 48(1) of the ERA 1996.

Parental leave rights

If an employee is able to satisfy the relevant requirements and procedures in regulations 13 and 15 of, and Schedule 2 to, the MPLR 1999, he is entitled to be absent from work on unpaid parental leave for the purpose of caring for a child under 18 years of age. The main condition is that the employee has a minimum of one year's continuous service with his/her employer. The period of parental leave is fixed at a maximum of 18 weeks and the decision in *Rodway* v *South Central Trains Ltd (formerly South Central Trains)* (2005) is an authority for the proposition that it is not possible for an employee to take less than one week's parental leave. An employee has no right to take more than four weeks' leave in any annual period. Sections 47C and 80 of the ERA 1996 direct that an employee may present a complaint to an employment tribunal where the employer has prevented him or her or attempted to prevent him or her from taking parental leave.

■ Rights under the Part-Time Workers (Prevention of Less Favourable Treatment) Regulations 2000

In terms of regulation 5(1) of the Part-Time Workers (Prevention of Less Favourable Treatment) Regulations 2000 (PTWR 2000), a part-time worker has the right not to suffer:

- less favourable treatment than a full-time worker (i.e. direct discrimination); or
- a detriment, solely for the reason that he or she is a part-time worker.

The source of the rights in the PTWR 2000 is EC Directive 97/81/EC of 15 December 1997 concerning the Framework Agreement on part-time work. The right under regulation 5(1) of the PTWR 2000 applies only if the less favourable treatment is:

- on the ground that the worker is a part-time worker;
- not justified on objective grounds, i.e. that the employer cannot demonstrate that the treatment or action which results in a detriment is a proportionate means of achieving a legitimate aim.

In terms of regulation 8(1) of the PTWR 2000, any infringement of regulation 5 is enforceable by presenting a complaint to an employment tribunal.

Matthews v *Kent and Medway Towns Fire Authority* **[2006] IRLR 367**

Concerning: reg. 5 of the PTWR 2000, appropriate comparator

Facts

Retained part-time fire-fighters argued that they were engaged in the same or broadly similar work as full-time fire-fighters working for the same employer. They also contended that both retained and full-time fire-fighters had the same type of contract described in terms of regulation 2(3)(a) of the PTWR 2000.

Legal principle

The House of Lords held that one had to look at the work that both the full-time worker and the part-time worker were engaged in and ask whether it was the same work or was broadly similar. The fact that the job of the full-time fire-fighter was a fuller, wider job than that of the retained fire-fighter was not a deciding factor. One had to address the question posed by the statute, which was whether the work on which both groups were engaged in could nevertheless be described as broadly similar. Accordingly, it was not open to the employment tribunal to conclude that the work of the full-time fire-fighter was not comparable with that of the retained fire-fighter.

■ Rights under the Fixed-Term Employees (Prevention of Less Favourable Treatment) Regulations 2002

The source of the rights in the Fixed-Term Employees (Prevention of Less Favourable Treatment) Regulations 2002 (FTER 2002) is EC Directive 1999/70/EC of 28 June 1999 concerning the framework agreement on fixed-term work. Like the PTWR 2000, regulation 3(1) of the FTER 2002 provides that a fixed-term employee has the right not to suffer:

- less favourable treatment than a permanent employee (i.e. direct discrimination); or
- a detriment, solely for the reason that he or she is a fixed-term employee.

The right under FTER 2002, regulation 3(3) applies only if the less favourable treatment is:

- on the ground that the employee is a fixed-term employee;
- not justified on objective grounds, i.e. that the employer cannot demonstrate that the treatment or action which results in a detriment is a proportionate means of achieving a legitimate aim.

Regulation 7(1) of FTER 2002 states that regulation 3 can be enforced by presenting a complaint to an employment tribunal.

■ Putting it all together

Answer guidelines

See the problem question at the start of this chapter. A diagram illustrating how to structure your answer is available on the website.

Approaching the question

This question requires you to describe and analyse the four separate claims which are available to Michael. It is crucial that you deal with each in turn in your answer. See below for further details.

Important points to include

Points to remember when answering this question:

- In your introduction, make the point that Michael has three heads of claim open to him.
- You should consider whether Michael has a claim on the basis that his employer has breached regulation 4(1) and (2) of WTR 1998. How can Michael enforce this claim?
- Address the issue of the statutory minimum periods of notice to which Michael is entitled and the effect of these entitlements.
- Examine whether Michael has a statutory right to know why he has been dismissed.

 Make your answer stand out

Analyse important case law which interprets the relevant piece of legislation, e.g. Barber v *RJB Mining (UK) Ltd* (1999) and *Sayers* v *Cambridgeshire County Council* (2007).

READ TO IMPRESS

Barnard, C., Deakin, S. and Hobbs, R. (2003) Opting out of the 48-hour week: employer necessity or individual choice? An empirical study of the operation of Article 18(1)(b) of the Working Time Directive in the UK. 32 *Industrial Law Journal*: 223.

Bogg, A. (2009) Of holidays, work and humanisation: a missed opportunity? 34 *European Law Review*: 738.

Davidov, G. (2009) A purposive interpretation of the National Minimum Wage Act. 72 *Modern Law Review*: 581.

Edwards, A. (2009) *Barber* v *RJB Mining* in the wider context of Health and Safety legislation. 9 *Industrial Law Journal*: 280.

Rodgers, L. (2009) The notion of working time. 38 *Industrial Law Journal*: 80.

Simpson, B. (2004) The National Minimum Wage five years on: reflections on some general issues. 33 *Industrial Law Journal*: 22.

Simpson, B. (2009) The Employment Act 2008's amendments to the National Minimum Wage legislation. 38 *Industrial Law Journal*: 57.

Mitchell, G. (2015) Encouraging fathers to care: The Children and Families Act 2014 and Shared Parental Leave. 44 *Industrial Law Journal*: 123.

www.pearsoned.co.uk/lawexpress

Go online to access more revision support including quizzes to test your knowledge, sample questions with answer guidelines, podcasts you can download, and more!

Discrimination in employment (1)

Revision checklist

Essential points you should know:

- [ ] The definition of the protected characteristics
- [ ] The definition of direct discrimination and how it is applied
- [ ] The definition of indirect discrimination and how it is applied
- [ ] An understanding of the concepts of harassment and sexual harassment
- [ ] An understanding of discrimination by way of victimisation

■ Topic map

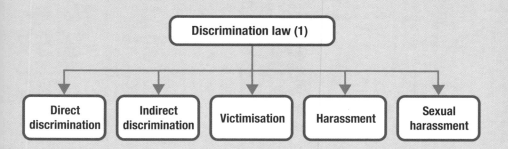

■ Introduction

An employee has the statutory right not to be discriminated against on the grounds of sex, race, disability, religious beliefs, philosophical beliefs, sexual orientation, marital/civil partnership status, pregnancy, maternity, gender reassignment or age.

Anti-discrimination legislation is one of the key planks upon which the EU's and the British Government's goal of achieving equality and diversity in the workplace is based. This chapter examines the principle of non-discrimination and examines the key components of such a principle as follows:

- direct discrimination;
- indirect discrimination;
- harassment;
- sexual harassment;
- victimisation.

In Chapter 6, we will explore:

- the remedies available to an employee who has suffered discrimination;
- the exceptions to the non-discrimination principle;
- the burden of proof in discrimination cases;
- aspects of disability discrimination and age discrimination in a greater amount of detail – since part of the disability and age discrimination regimes do not fully mirror the pattern established in the cases of sex, race, religious belief and sexual orientation discrimination legislation.

ASSESSMENT ADVICE

Essay questions

Essay questions require broad general knowledge of the key concepts in anti-discrimination legislation, such as direct discrimination, indirect discrimination, victimisation, harassment and sexual harassment. You should be able to explore each of these key concepts and to critically evaluate them. You should also be able to identify the elements of the key concepts which can be used as a defence by an employer. In tackling essay questions, you should always directly answer the question(s) asked and apply the relevant law.

▶

Problem questions

These may give a set of facts relative to individual employees and ask you to advise them whether they have a reasonable prospect of success in presenting a complaint to an employment tribunal on the basis of the anti-discrimination legislation. Such questions seek to identify your understanding of the key concepts in the legislation and how an employer may be able to raise a defence. In tackling problem questions, you should always directly answer the question(s) asked and apply the relevant law to the facts at hand. For example, if a problem question states that a female employee suffers from unwanted sexual advances from male colleagues, you should seek to ascertain whether the concept of sexual harassment in section 26(2) of the Equality Act 2010 is satisfied.

■ Sample question

Could you answer this question? Below is a typical essay question that could arise on this topic. Guidelines on answering the question are included at the end of the chapter, while a sample problem question and guidance on tackling it can be found on the companion website.

ESSAY QUESTION

Identify the four components of the test of indirect discrimination under the Equality Act 2010. Explain how each of these components might be used by an employer to defend an indirect discrimination claim.

■ The scope of discrimination law in the employment field

Anti-discrimination provisions cover the whole spectrum of the employment relationship, from selection and recruitment to promotion, transfer and dismissal.

KEY STATUTE

Equality Act 2010 (EA 2010), s. 39

(1) An employer (A) must not discriminate against a person (B) –
   (a) in the arrangements A makes for deciding to whom to offer employment;
   (b) as to the terms on which A offers B employment;
   (c) by not offering B employment.

(2) An employer (A) must not discriminate against an employee of A's (B) –

    (a) as to B's terms of employment;

    (b) in the way A affords B access, or by not affording B access, to opportunities for promotion, transfer or training or for receiving any other benefit, facility or service;

    (c) by dismissing B;

    (d) by subjecting B to any other detriment.

■ Definitions

The EA 2010 refers to 'protected characteristics' which are listed as the following in section 4 of the EA 2010: age, **disability**, gender reassignment, marriage and civil partnership, pregnancy and maternity, race, religion or belief, sex and sexual orientation. The definitions of race, religion or belief, sex and sexual orientation, which are relevant to an essay or problem question, are as follows:

KEY STATUTE

EA 2010, s. 9

(1) Race includes –

    (a) colour;

    (b) nationality;

    (c) ethnic or national origins. . .

(3) A racial group is a group of persons defined by reference to race; and a reference to a person's racial group is a reference to a racial group into which the person falls.

EA 2010, s. 10

(1) Religion means any religion and a reference to religion includes a reference to a lack of religion.

(2) Belief means any religious or philosophical belief and a reference to belief includes a reference to a lack of belief.

EA 2010, s. 11

In relation to the protected characteristic of sex –

(a) a reference to a person who has a particular protected characteristic is a reference to a man or to a woman;

(b) a reference to persons who share a protected characteristic is a reference to persons of the same sex.

▶

EA 2010, s. 12

(1) Sexual orientation means a person's sexual orientation towards –

    (a) persons of the same sex,
    (b) persons of the opposite sex, or
    (c) persons of either sex.

📖 **REVISION NOTE**

The definition of disability in section 6 of the EA 2010 will be considered separately in Chapter 6.

'Racial group'?

In *Mandla* v *Dowell Lee* (1983), the House of Lords held that Sikhs were a 'racial group' within the meaning of section 9(3) of the EA 2010. Sikhs were a 'racial group' since they satisfied the following essential conditions:

- they had a long shared history, distinguishing them from other groups;
- they had a unique cultural tradition;
- they had a common geographical origin or descent from a small number of common ancestors;
- they had a common language;
- they had a common literary heritage;
- they had a common religion distinguishing them from neighbouring groups;
- they were a minority group.

Meanwhile, in *Dawkins* v *Crown Suppliers* (1993) the Court of Appeal held that where there is no group language or descent and the group is essentially a religious sect, such as Rastafarians, section 9(3) of the EA 2010 will not have been satisfied. In the case of *R* v *Governing Body of Jews Free School* (2010), the Supreme Court interpreted 'ethnic origin' in section 9(1) of the EA 2010 even more widely, holding that a person will have been subjected to unlawful discrimination on ethnic grounds if he is discriminated against on grounds of who he is descended from. It has been held in *Chandhok* v *Tirkey* (2015) that caste falls within the scope of section 9 of the EA 2010.

'Religious or philosophical belief'?

Regulation 2(1) of the Employment Equality (Religion or Belief) Regulations 2003 (SI 2003/1660) originally defined 'religion or belief' as 'any religion, religious belief, or similar philosophical belief'. To that extent, a philosophical belief had to be similar in nature to a religious belief in order to fall within the scope of regulation 2. However, section 10 of the EA 2010 now has a different definition of 'religion' and 'belief'. Indeed, 'philosophical belief' is set apart from 'religion' or 'belief' and the word 'similar' has been removed. Therefore, there is no longer any requirement for a philosophical belief to share affinities with a religious belief.

> **❗ Don't be tempted to . . .**
>
> You should not fall into the trap of thinking that a particular person cannot fall within the scope of more than one protected characteristic. Sometimes a group will enjoy protection under both the definitions of 'race' and 'religion' in sections 9 and 10 of the EA 2010. Another point worth noting is that the words 'religious or philosophical belief' in section 10 of the EA 2010 appear to be wide enough to include groups such as Rastafarians.

◼ The prohibition of direct discrimination

The prohibition of direct discrimination is geared towards the eradication of unfavourable treatment of individuals forming part of a group in the workplace on the basis that they form part of that group. The legislation envisages persons being treated according to their merits, skills, qualities and defects. See Figure 5.1 for a breakdown of the approach to direct discrimination.

Figure 5.1

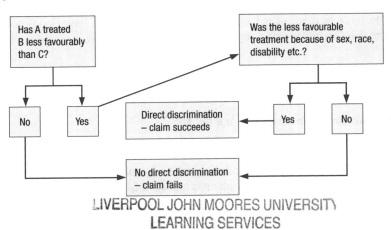

KEY STATUTE

EA 2010, s. 13

(1) A person (A) discriminates against another (B) if, because of a protected characteristic, A treats B less favourably than A treats or would treat others. . .

(5) If the protected characteristic is race, less favourable treatment includes segregating B from others.

(6) If the protected characteristic is sex –

 (a) less favourable treatment of a woman includes less favourable treatment of her because she is breast-feeding;

 (b) in a case where B is a man, no account is to be taken of special treatment afforded to a woman in connection with pregnancy or childbirth.

! Don't be tempted to . . .

Don't be fooled into thinking that because the employer's proportionality defence is available to the employer in the case of the protected characteristic of age it must also apply in the case of direct sex, race, disability, pregnancy, maternity, marriage, civil partnership, gender reassignment, religion, belief and sexual orientation discrimination. In these cases, you should keep in mind the fact that subject to the possibility of arguing that a genuine occupational requirement applies (see Chapter 6), the employer does not have a statutory defence.

'Less favourable treatment'

For the purposes of establishing 'less favourable treatment' and direct discrimination, a series of cases have decided that the motives, intention, policy reasons or criteria of an employer in discriminating are irrelevant. Originally, the courts took the view that whether there had been 'less favourable treatment' was primarily an issue of causation, i.e. a 'but for' test. The law has now changed. In the case of *R* v *Governing Body of Jews Free School* (2010), the Supreme Court ruled that a 'reason why' test is now applicable.

KEY CASE

James v *Eastleigh Borough Council* **[1990] IRLR 288**

Concerning: 'less favourable treatment', 'but for' test

Facts

Mr and Mrs James were both aged 61. Mr James made a complaint that he had to pay to gain entrance to a council swimming pool whereas his wife did not.

Entrance to the swimming pool was free for women aged 60 or over and men aged 65 or over.

Legal principle

The House of Lords held that Mr James had suffered direct discrimination. Building on its earlier jurisprudence in *R v Birmingham County Council, ex p EOC* (1989), the House of Lords held that there was direct discrimination and less favourable treatment on the ground of sex if Mr James would have received the same treatment as females but for his sex. Thus, a 'but for' test was applied.

□ REVISION NOTE

See Figure 5.1, which describes the standard pattern of how an employee can satisfy a direct discrimination claim. However, you should recall that direct age discrimination does not exactly follow the standard direct discrimination pattern (see Chapter 6).

KEY CASE

R v Governing Body of Jews Free School [2010] IRLR 136

Concerning: 'less favourable treatment', 'reason why' test

Facts

The admissions policy of the Jews Free School (JFS) prescribed that preference ought to be given to children recognised as Orthodox Jews by the Office of the Chief Rabbi (OCR). The OCR's criteria were that a child would be treated as Orthodox Jewish if the mother of the child was an Orthodox Jew either by matrilineal descent or by conversion. Admission to the JFS was denied to a child on the grounds that his Italian mother was formerly a Roman Catholic and a convert to Masorti Judaism, which was a denomination not recognised by the OCR. The father raised proceedings against the JFS on the basis that his son had suffered direct and indirect racial discrimination under the provisions of the Race Relations Act 1976, which were then in force.

Legal principle

The Supreme Court held that the child had been the victim of direct racial discrimination on the basis of a lack of a particular ethnic origin. He had been less favourably treated than others for the reason of his mother's ethnic origins, which were Italian and Roman Catholic, and her lack of ethnic origin as an Orthodox Jew. As for the proper approach to a direct discrimination claim, the majority of the Supreme Court took the view that where it is established that there has been less favourable treatment, but the factual ▶

criterion or criteria which influenced the employer to act in the way that it did are not inherently discriminatory or plain on their face, it is incumbent upon the tribunal or court to explore the mental processes of the alleged discriminator, i.e. to examine the reason why the employer might have acted in the way that it did on the basis of an objective test. Hence, the courts must ascertain the 'reason why' the employer acted in the way that it did when it is unclear what motivated the employer, but in doing so, a subjective test is not applied. Therefore, the evidence of the employer as to what it intended, what motivated it and its reasons are irrelevant and the court must determine the 'reason why' from an objective standpoint. In other words, it will be helpful for a court to ask whether there was less favourable treatment, and if so, whether such less favourable treatment was on the grounds of sex.

The requirement for a 'comparator'

It is open to an employee to compare himself or herself with a hypothetical comparator for the purposes of establishing whether there has been 'less favourable treatment'. This will be necessary where no actual comparator in the workplace can be identified. In selecting a fictitious comparator, a comparison of the cases must be such that the relevant circumstances in the one case are the same, or not materially different, in the other case – see EA 2010, section 23(1).

◼ The prohibition of indirect discrimination

Indirect discrimination covers the situation where an employer applies a criterion or practice to all of its employees generally, of a particular class, which by definition indirectly affects or prejudices certain groups of employees. The effect is called 'disparate impact'. There are four components to an indirect discrimination claim:

- a provision, criterion or practice must have been applied;
- particular group disadvantage must be established;
- disadvantage to the claimant must be established;
- the employer must not be able to show that the application of the provision, criterion or practice was proportionate.

KEY STATUTE

EA 2010, s. 19

(1) A person (A) discriminates against another (B) if A applies to B a provision, criterion or practice which is discriminatory in relation to a relevant protected characteristic of B's.

> (2) For the purposes of subsection (1), a provision, criterion or practice is discriminatory in relation to a relevant protected characteristic of B's if –
>   (a) A applies, or would apply, it to persons with whom B does not share the characteristic,
>   (b) it puts, or would put, persons with whom B shares the characteristic at a particular disadvantage when compared with persons with whom B does not share it,
>   (c) it puts, or would put, B at that disadvantage, and
>   (d) A cannot show it to be a proportionate means of achieving a legitimate aim.

Dissecting the test of indirect discrimination

The current incarnation of the test of indirect discrimination is set out in Figure 5.2, which describes the mechanics of indirect discrimination from the perspective of a claim which is based on the protected characteristic of sex.

'Provision, criterion or practice'

These words replaced the words 'requirement or condition' which originally featured in the Sex Discrimination Act 1975 and the Race Relations Act 1976. The words 'requirement or condition' required the claimant to identify an absolute bar imposed by the employer upon compliance – *Perera* v *Civil Service Commission (No. 2)* (1983). This was an exceptionally high hurdle for complainants to meet and so the law was relaxed:

- in 2001 (by the Sex Discrimination (Indirect Discrimination and Burden of Proof) Regulations 2001 (SI 2001/2660));
- again on 1 October 2005 (by the Employment Equality (Sex Discrimination) Regulations 2005 (SI 2005/2467)). What is now found in section 19 of the EA 2010 is more or less identical to what was introduced by these reforms in 2005.

Hence, instead of being required to identify an absolute bar, the complainant is merely required to show a criterion, provision or practice which affects him or her.

'Particular disadvantage' – selection of a pool for comparison

In determining whether members (including the claimant) of a certain sex, race, religion, belief, sexual orientation, disability or age are put at a 'particular disadvantage' when compared with others who do not share that protected characteristic, a pool for comparison must be identified. The pools selected must be such that the relevant circumstances in one

Figure 5.2

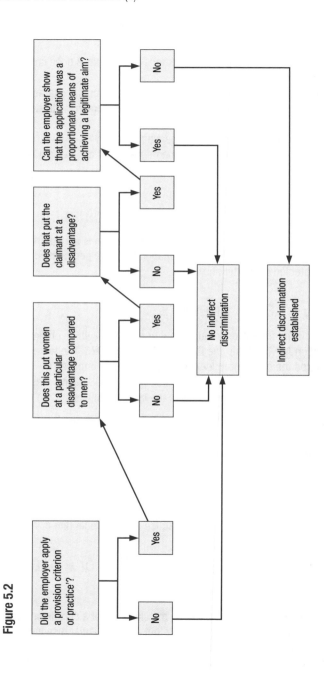

case are the same, or not materially different, in the other: section 23 of the EA 2010. In other words, a class of persons against whom a comparison can be made must be chosen in order to establish whether the complainant and the group of which the complainant forms part have been put at a particular disadvantage by the application of the provision, criterion or practice. Challenges to the suitability of one pool over others are a common feature of the cases.

KEY CASE

Jones v *University of Manchester* [1993] IRLR 218

Concerning: suitability of 'pool' for comparison

Facts

The university advertised a post for a careers adviser. The person appointed was required to be a graduate, preferably between 27 and 35 years of age. Ms Jones who applied for the post was aged 46. She was not shortlisted on the basis of her age and she complained that the university's requirements indirectly discriminated against women who were mature students.

Legal principle

The Court of Appeal rejected Ms Jones's complaint. In the present case, Ms Jones's case was directed to proving:

- not that the proportion of women graduates who could comply with the age requirement was considerably smaller than the proportion of male graduates who could comply with it – as required by the statute
- but instead that the proportion of women mature graduates who could comply with the age requirement was considerably smaller – which is not what was required by the statute.

! Don't be tempted to . . .

Be careful about invoking the relevance of statistics as a means of showing that a group is suffering from a 'particular disadvantage'. Before the 2005 reforms, the complainant was required to show that a 'considerably smaller proportion' of the allegedly disadvantaged group could comply with the condition applied. This has been softened to the 'particular disadvantage' test, which leaves a larger margin for error when statistics are considered. Thus, it is now the case that the scope for statistical discrepancies to defeat the complainant's case has been considerably reduced since the complainant need only demonstrate that some – not all – of the group are disadvantaged by the application of the provision, criterion or practice.

Proportionality – the employer's defence

The employer has a proportionality defence. In considering whether the employer's application of a provision, criterion or practice is a 'proportionate means of achieving a legitimate aim', the first thing for the employer to identify is its legitimate aim. It is then for the courts and tribunals to consider whether that aim is indeed 'legitimate' on the basis of an objective test. If it is found to be legitimate, then the court and tribunal must ask whether the application of the provision, criterion or practice is a proportionate response to the achievement of that legitimate aim. It is inherent in the principle of proportionality that where different means of achieving a particular objective could be adapted, the one which has the least discriminatory impact should be chosen by the employer. This is known as the 'least restrictive means' test, on which see *Bilka-Kaufhaus GmbH* v *Karin Weber von Hartz* (1986) and Baker (2008).

■ Harassment

There are now two forms of harassment prohibited by the EA 2010, section 26: first there is harassment, which is 'related to' a person's sex, race, disability, religion, belief, sexual orientation, gender reassignment and/or age: these are referred to as the 'relevant protected characteristics' in EA 2010, section 26. Secondly, there is sexual harassment, which is essentially harassment of a sexual nature.

Harassment 'related to' a relevant protected characteristic

KEY STATUTE

EA 2010, s. 26

(1)   A person (A) harasses another (B) if –

(a)   A engages in unwanted conduct related to a relevant protected characteristic, and

(b)   the conduct has the purpose or effect of –

(i)   violating B's dignity, or

(ii)   creating an intimidating, hostile, degrading, humiliating or offensive environment for B . . .

📖 REVISION NOTE

Article 2(1)(c) of the Recast Equality Directive 2006/54/EC (which applies to sex) defines harassment as 'where unwanted conduct related to the sex of a person occurs with the purpose or effect of violating the dignity of a person, and of creating an intimidating, hostile, degrading, humiliating or offensive treatment'. Instead of using the words 'related to the sex', section 4A of the now repealed Sex Discrimination Act 1975 initially employed the words 'on the ground of her sex'. In the case of *R (on the application of EOC)* v *Secretary of State for Trade and Industry* (2007), the High Court held that section 4A of the Sex Discrimination Act 1975 in that format did not adequately implement the Recast Equality Directive. This was on the basis that the words 'on the ground of her sex' required the claimant to compare herself with a member of the opposite sex as a means of establishing harassment, whereas the words 'related to the sex' in the Recast Equality Directive do not require such a comparison to be made. Since the decision in *R (on the application of EOC)* v *Secretary of State for Trade and Industry*, we now find the words 'related to' in section 26 of the EA 2010 which apply not only to sex but also to race, disability, religion, belief, sexual orientation, gender reassignment and/or age, i.e. the 'relevant protected characteristics'. Hence, there is no longer any requirement for a claimant complaining of harassment to compare himself or herself with a person falling within a group which does not share the relevant protected characteristic and to show that she was treated less favourably than that person. Moreover, discrimination/harassment by association is now outlawed, i.e. where an employer engages in conduct which is neither directed at the recipient nor the relevant protected characteristic of the recipient, such conduct may nevertheless amount to 'harassment related to' a relevant protected characteristic in contravention of section 26 if that conduct is prejudicial and relates to one of the relevant protected characteristics generally, e.g. where an employer makes a series of derogatory remarks about women or homosexuals generally such as to create an intimidating, hostile, degrading, humiliating or offensive environment for the employee.

Sexual harassment

KEY STATUTE

EA 2010, s. 26

(2)   A also harasses B if –

    (a)   A engages in unwanted conduct of a sexual nature, and

    (b)   the conduct has the purpose or effect [of violating B's dignity or of creating an intimidating, hostile, degrading, humiliating or offensive environment for B].

!   Don't be tempted to . . .

You should avoid referring to comparators in the context of the concept of harassment. Although the words 'conduct of a sexual nature' in section 26(2)(a) of the EA 2010 are not defined and there is no practical guidance as to what kind of conduct falls within these words, what is clear is that a woman or man alleging sexual harassment on the basis of section 26(2)(a) of the EA 2010 will not require to compare herself or himself with a member of the opposite sex. For further issues arising, see Clarke (2006).

You should be clear that you understand the difference between:

(a) harassment of a sexual nature, and

(b) harassment related to a relevant protected characteristic.

In particular, you should appreciate the difference between sexual harassment and harassment related to sex, as these two things are not the same. In a problem question, where the harassing conduct is sexual-neutral, but is directed at a particular gender, it is more likely that (b) above will be relevant. On the other hand, if the conduct is of a sexual nature, e.g. offensive remarks, jokes or pictures, stalking or inappropriate physical contact, it is more likely that (a) is relevant.

■ Victimisation

B is victimised under section 27 of the EA 2010 if A subjects B to a detriment because B has done a protected act or A believes that B has done, or may do, a protected act. Each of the following is a protected act:

(a) B has brought proceedings against A under the EA 2010;

(b) B has given evidence or information in connection with such proceedings;

(c) B has done anything for the purposes of or in connection with the EA 2010; or

(d) B alleged that A or any other person has committed an act which would amount to a contravention of the EA 2010.

In the case of *Derbyshire* v *St Helens Metropolitan Borough Council* (2007), the House of Lords decided that, under the victimisation provisions, it is primarily from the perspective of the alleged victim that the question whether or not any 'detriment' had been suffered will be determined, i.e. victimisation is not to be judged from the point of view of the alleged discriminator. However, there is an argument that the word 'because' in section 27 of the EA 2010 requires consideration of the reason why the employer had done the particular act, and to that extent the alleged act of victimisation has to be assessed from the employer's viewpoint.

In the context of problem questions, you should look out for facts which suggest that a worker is suffering some kind of detriment as a result of his or her gender, race, etc. Sometimes, the problem question will state that the victimisation or detriment has been threatened by the employer – you should be clear that such threats will also be covered within the statutory definition of victimisation.

■ Putting it all together

Answer guidelines

See the essay question at the start of this chapter. A diagram illustrating how to structure your answer is available on the website.

Approaching the question

This question requires you to describe and analyse the four elements that make up an indirect discrimination claim. It is crucial that you deal with each in turn in your answer. See below for further details.

Important points to include

Points to remember when answering this question:

■ You should be able to demonstrate that you appreciate that the definition of indirect discrimination has changed a number of times since 2001.

■ You must address the meaning of the phrase 'provision, criterion or practice'.

■ How do the courts and tribunals assess whether a group is placed at a 'particular disadvantage'?

■ An exploration of the employer's proportionality defence is paramount – how does this operate in practice?

 Make your answer stand out

You should be able to examine the differences between the current test of 'indirect discrimination' and the previous tests of indirect discrimination that referred to a 'requirement or condition' and a 'considerably smaller proportion', etc.

Does the application of the new test of indirect discrimination in section 19 of the EA 2010 make it slightly easier for claimants to be successful?

READ TO IMPRESS

Baker, A. (2008) Proportionality and employment discrimination in the UK. 37 *Industrial Law Journal*: 30.

Bowers, J. and Moran, A. (2002) Justification in direct sex discrimination law: breaking the taboo. 31 *Industrial Law Journal*: 307.

Bowers, J. and Moran, A. (2003) Justification in direct sex discrimination law: a reply. 32 *Industrial Law Journal*: 185.

Clarke, L. (2006) Harassment, sexual harassment, and the Employment Equality (Sex Discrimination) Regulations 2005. 35 *Industrial Law Journal*: 161.

Connolly, M. (2010) Racial groups, sub-groups, the demise of the *But For* Test and the death of the benign motive defence: *R (on the application of E)* v *Governing Body of JFS*. 39 *Industrial Law Journal*: 183.

Finnis, J. (2010) Directly discriminatory decisions: a missed opportunity? 126 *Law Quarterly Review*: 491.

Gill, T. and Monaghan, K. (2003) Justification in direct sex discrimination law: taboo upheld. 32(2) *Industrial Law Journal*: 115.

www.pearsoned.co.uk/lawexpress

Go online to access more revision support including quizzes to test your knowledge, sample questions with answer guidelines, podcasts you can download, and more!

Discrimination in employment (2)

6

Revision checklist

Essential points you should know:

- [ ] That there are statutory exceptions to the principle of non-discrimination
- [ ] The burden of proof in discrimination cases
- [ ] The meaning of 'discrimination arising from disability'
- [ ] When an employer must make 'reasonable adjustments' in the context of a disability discrimination claim
- [ ] The key concepts applicable in the context of age discrimination

■ Topic map

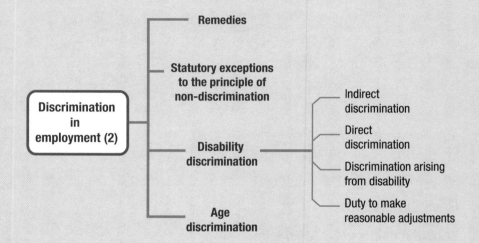

■ Introduction

The Equality Act 2010 (EA 2010) prohibits discrimination arising from disability, direct disability discrimination and indirect disability discrimination and imposes a duty to make reasonable adjustments.

In this chapter, we will explore the remedies available to an employee who has succeeded in a discrimination claim, and the exceptions to the principle of non-discrimination in the case of sex, disability, race, religion, philosophical belief, sexual orientation, marital/civil partnership status, pregnancy, maternity, gender reassignment or age, i.e. where it is lawful to discriminate against employees falling within such groups. The burden of proof also needs to be considered. Finally, some of the concepts which are unique to the disability and age discrimination regimes will be examined.

ASSESSMENT ADVICE

Essay questions

Essay questions require broad general knowledge of the remedies available to an employee pursuant to the anti-discrimination legislation and the exceptions to the anti-discrimination principle. An issue which is very topical is the burden of proof in discrimination cases. Moreover, discrimination arising from disability and the duty to make reasonable adjustments may be assessed and a firm grasp of how the courts and tribunals approach these issues is paramount. In tackling essay questions, you should always directly answer the question(s) asked and apply the relevant law.

Problem questions

These may require you to assess whether an employer has a defence to a sex, race, religion, etc. discrimination claim based on the application of one of the statutory exceptions in the EA 2010. As for discrimination claims made on the ground of disability, you may be asked to assess whether a claim based on the test of 'discrimination arising from disability' or the employer's duty to make reasonable adjustments is likely to be successful or not. In tackling problem questions, you should always directly answer the question(s) asked and apply the relevant law to the facts at hand. For example, if a problem question provides that an employee in a wheelchair is unable to gain access to some part of her employer's premises, you should look to ascertain whether the employer's statutory duty to make reasonable adjustments in sections 20 to 22 of the EA 2010 has been breached.

Sample question

Could you answer this question? Below is a typical problem question that could arise on this topic. Guidelines on answering the question are included at the end of the chapter, while a sample essay question and guidance on tackling it can be found on the companion website.

PROBLEM QUESTION

Kashif Rao is a salesman working for a firm of computer software and hardware manufacturers. He is paid a very low basic salary of £8,000 per annum and the majority of his remuneration is made up of commission on sales, performance-related pay and bonuses. His job involves travelling by motor vehicle to clients of his employer located throughout the northern counties of England. After a minor road accident, he suffers from severe back pains when he drives a motor car for more than two hours at a time. His consultant's prognosis is that he suffers from a condition which is likely to have a long-term and substantial adverse effect on his ability to perform his duties since he is likely to suffer such severe back pains for the rest of his life. He is upset when his employer refuses to (i) provide him with additional breaks during his working day and (ii) modify his contractual remuneration structure. Advise Kashif.

Remedies

The remedies available to an employee who has succeeded in a discrimination claim are set out in section 124 of the EA 2010 and are as follows:

- a declaration as to the rights of the employee and employer in relation to the matters to which the proceedings relates;
- an order requiring the employer to pay compensation to the employee; or
- a recommendation that the employer take certain specified steps within a specified period for the purpose of obviating or reducing the adverse effect of any matter to which the proceedings relate.

Calculation of compensation

In the majority of cases in which an employee is successful in a discrimination claim, compensation will be the remedy awarded by the employment tribunal. Unlike the remedy of compensation in the case of unfair dismissal, there is no cap on the amount which may be awarded to a successful employee. Indeed, awards of compensation can vary significantly. Where an employee or employer fails to follow the Equality Act 2010 Code of Practice on Employment of the Equality and Human Rights Commission (EHRC) (see http://equalityhumanrights.com/uploaded_files/EqualityAct/employercode.pdf), the employment tribunal may reduce or increase the award of compensation by up to 25 per cent in terms of section 207A of, and Schedule A2 to, the Trade Union and Labour Relations (Consolidation) Act 1992. A substantial percentage of the award will represent injury to the employee's feelings in suffering the discrimination, harassment or victimisation. In the cases of *Vento* v *Chief Constable of West Yorkshire Police (No. 2)* (2003) and *Da'Bell* v *National Society for the Prevention of Cruelty to Children* (2010), the Court of Appeal and Employment Appeal Tribunal offered guidance on the range of awards for injury to feelings:

- awards of between £500 and £6,000 should be made for less serious cases, e.g. where the discrimination, harassment or victimisation is an isolated incident;
- awards of between £6,000 and £18,000 ought to be made for more serious cases, e.g. where there is a course of conduct amounting to discrimination, harassment or victimisation;
- awards of between £18,000 and £30,000 should be made for the most serious cases where there has been a concerted campaign of discrimination, victimisation and harassment. However, only in exceptional circumstances should the award for injury to feelings be more than £30,000.

■ 'Genuine occupational requirement' exceptions

Schedule 9 to the EA 2010 contains certain provisions called 'genuine occupational requirements'. These provisions represent statutory exceptions to the general principle of non-discrimination where the employer is able to show that the application of that requirement is a proportionate means of achieving a legitimate aim. Essentially, they enable the employer to engage in discriminatory activity where one of the exceptions applies. These exceptions are restricted to certain factual categories. With the exception of the protected characteristics of religion, belief and age, there is no precise indication in Schedule 9 to the EA 2010 as to what will constitute genuine occupational requirements. This can be contrasted with the equality legislation in force prior to the introduction of the EA 2010 where specific examples of genuine occupational requirements were given, e.g. sections 4A and 5 of the Race Relations Act 1976 and section 7 of the Sex Discrimination Act 1975. Section 7 of the Sex Discrimination Act 1975 stipulated that it was lawful to insist on a job being fulfilled by a man where this was required:

- for reasons of physiology (excluding physical strength or stamina);
- for reasons of authenticity, e.g. theatrical performers, actors and entertainers;

- for reasons of the preservation of decency or privacy; and/or
- in the context of a hospital, prison, residential care unit or nursing home.

It should be stressed that p. 172 of the Equality Act 2010 Code of Practice on Employment of the EHRC (see http://equalityhumanrights.com/uploaded_files/EqualityAct/employercode.pdf) is drafted in such a way as to suggest that the above examples are likely to be of continued relevance where the protected characteristic is sex.

✎ EXAM TIP

In Chapter 5, you were introduced to the key concepts contained in anti-discrimination legislation such as direct discrimination, indirect discrimination, harassment and victimisation. A problem question may include facts which point towards a case of discrimination on one of these bases. However, the facts may concern someone employed (or seeking employment) as a theatrical performer, actor or in a prison, hospital or female nursing home (where there is scope for segregation of the sexes). Here, you should consider whether the genuine occupational requirements exceptions may apply to defeat a complainant's discrimination claim.

■ Burden of proof

Once a complainant has established certain facts from which a tribunal could conclude that the employer has committed an act of discrimination or harassment, the onus of proof shifts to the employer to show that it has not committed such an act of discrimination or harassment.

The application of the burden of proof test in practice has resulted in a great deal of litigation. See *Igen Ltd* v *Wong* (2005).

KEY STATUTE

EA 2010, s. 136

(1) This section applies to any proceedings relating to a contravention of this Act.

(2) If there are facts from which the court could decide, in the absence of any other explanation, that a person (A) contravened the provision concerned, the court must hold that the contravention occurred.

(3) But subsection (2) does not apply if A shows that A did not contravene the provision.

(4) The reference to a contravention of this Act includes a reference to a breach of an equality clause or rule . . .

(6) A reference to the court includes a reference to –

    (a) an employment tribunal . . .

KEY CASE

Igen Ltd v *Wong* **[2005] IRLR 258**

Concerning: burden of proof, anti-discrimination legislation

Facts

This case considered whether the guidance of the EAT in *Barton* v *Investec Henderson Crosthwaite Securities Ltd* (2003) ought to be applied or not.

Legal principle

The Court of Appeal held that EA 2010, section 136 required an employment tribunal to apply the following two-stage process if a complaint were to be upheld:

(1) the complainant must prove facts from which the tribunal could conclude (in the absence of an adequate explanation from the employer) that the employer had committed, or was to be treated as having committed, the unlawful act of discrimination against the complainant; and

(2) the second stage, which only comes into effect if the complainant has proved those facts, requires the employer to prove that he has not committed, or is not to be treated as having committed, the unlawful act. In order to do this, it is necessary for the employer to prove, on the balance of probabilities, that the treatment was in no sense whatsoever attributable to a protected characteristic, i.e. sex, race, etc.

At the first stage, the tribunal must assume that the employer has advanced no adequate explanation for the primary facts proved by the complainant. At the second stage, the burden of proof has clearly shifted to the employer to the effect that it must provide an adequate explanation.

Further guidance on stages 1 and 2

Igen Ltd v *Wong* (2005) established the two-stage test. However, some questions remained unanswered and have been subsequently resolved in respect of stage 1:

■ In *Laing* v *Manchester City Council* (2006), the EAT held that at stage 1, an employment tribunal is entitled to take into account all material facts (which can be distinguished from an adequate explanation advanced by the employer) in coming to a view.

■ In *Brown* v *London Borough of Croydon* (2007), where the claimant is comparing herself or himself against a hypothetical comparator, the Court of Appeal held that it is good practice to apply the two-stage test, but that it is not an error of law for a tribunal to move straight to stage 2 without considering stage 1. Such an approach does not prejudice the employee.

- In *Madarassy* v *Nomura International plc* (2007), the Court of Appeal held that, in order to satisfy stage 1, an employee must show more than:

    (a) a mere difference in sex or other protected characteristic between herself and the comparator (real or hypothetical);

    (b) a mere difference of treatment between herself and the comparator (real or hypothetical).

Hence, (a) a difference in sex or another protected characteristic + (b) a difference in treatment does not necessarily = the satisfaction of stage 1. All that (a) + (b) demonstrates is a possibility of discrimination and more evidence is required from the employee.

📖 REVISION NOTE

The cases dealing with the burden of proof are very important for the purposes of the test of direct discrimination. If you compare the two-stage 'reason why' approach applied in the context of direct discrimination (see Chapter 5), it becomes clear that it mirrors the two-stage test in the case of the burden of proof. In other words, at stage 1, the onus lies on the employee to prove that the employee has suffered less favourable treatment or was to be treated as having suffered less favourable treatment. Thereafter, at stage 2, the burden shifts to the employer to prove that the 'reason why' was in no sense whatsoever to do with the employee's sex, race, disability, etc., i.e. a genuine non-discriminatory reason.

◼ Disability discrimination

Disability

The definition of '**disability**' is contained in section 6 of the EA 2010.

KEY STATUTE

EA 2010, s. 6

(1) A person (P) has a disability if –

   (a) P has a physical or mental impairment, and
   (b) the impairment has a substantial and long-term adverse effect on P's ability to carry out normal day-to-day activities.

(2) A reference to a disabled person is a reference to a person who has a disability.

(3) In relation to the protected characteristic of disability –

   (a) a reference to a person who has a particular protected characteristic is a reference to a person who has a particular disability;
   (b) a reference to persons who share a protected characteristic is a reference to persons who have the same disability.

Figure 6.1

Key component no.	Nature of key component
1	'Mental impairment' or 'physical impairment';
2	which has a 'substantial adverse effect', on 'normal day-to-day activities'; and
3	'long-term adverse effect' on 'normal day-to-day activities'

See Figure 6.1 for the key components of 'disability'. In *Goodwin* v *Patent Office* (1999), the EAT divided the definition of 'disability' into four parts: (i) the impairment condition, (ii) the adverse effect condition, (iii) the substantial condition and (iv) the long-term condition.

Disability: further guidance

Schedule 1 to the EA 2010 and the Equality Act 2010 (Disability) Regulations 2010 (SI 2010/2128) provide further guidance as to what constitutes a 'disability'. For example, the words 'long-term effects' and 'substantial adverse effects' are defined and persons with cancer, HIV, MS and other prescribed conditions are deemed to be 'disabled'. The definitions of 'mental impairment' and 'physical impairment' in the EA 2010 are complemented by guidance issued by the EHRC, on which see the Equality Act 2010 Code of Practice on Employment of the Equality and Human Rights Commission (see http://equalityhumanrights. com/uploaded_files/EqualityAct/employercode.pdf). An important point is that it is not necessary to show that an employee is suffering from a well-recognised mental illness for that person to be suffering from a 'mental impairment'. Moreover, the effect of the decision of the ECJ in *Coleman* v *Attridge Law* (2008) is that associative discrimination is unlawful under the European Framework Directive 2000/78/EC of 27 November 2000, which prohibits disability discrimination in employment throughout the EU. That is to say those individuals, such as carers, who are associated with disabled persons have the right to be protected in respect of disability discrimination – even though the disabled person himself has not been discriminated against.

Types of disability discrimination

Apart from harassment and victimisation on the grounds of disability (both considered in Chapter 5), there are essentially four key forms of disability discrimination:

(a) the duty to make reasonable adjustments;

(b) discrimination arising from disability;

(c) direct disability discrimination (considered in Chapter 5);

(d) indirect disability discrimination (considered in Chapter 5).

A few points can be made on the interaction between (a), (b), (c) and (d) as follows:

■ and (c) can never be justified by an employer;

■ (a), (c) and (d) each involve the making of comparisons, but (b) does not: *Akerman-Livingstone* v *Aster Communities Ltd* (2015). In the case of (b), the disabled claimant does not require to be compared with a disabled or non-disabled person and so the approach of the House of Lords in *Mayor and Burgesses of the London Borough of Lewisham* v *Malcolm* (2008) is no longer applicable as this approach related to the predecessor statutory concept of 'disability-related discrimination' in section 3A(1) of the Disability Discrimination Act 1995 (DDA 1995), which is now repealed.

■ Meanwhile, for the purposes of (c) and (d), section 23 of the EA 2010 provides that the comparator (actual or hypothetical), must not be disabled and must have the same (or not materially different) relevant circumstances as the disabled person.

■ Moreover, for the purpose of (a), the case of *Smith* v *Churchills Stairlifts plc* (2006) held that the correct comparator is not the population as a whole, but those others who fulfil the other conditions for the job who are not disabled.

Duty to make reasonable adjustments

The employer's duty to make reasonable adjustments is set out in sections 20 and 21 of the EA 2010.

KEY STATUTE

EA 2010, s. 20

(1) Where this Act imposes a duty to make reasonable adjustments on a person, this section, sections 21 and 22 and [Schedule 8] apply; and for those purposes, a person on whom the duty is imposed is referred to as A.

(2) The duty comprises the following three requirements.

(3) The first requirement is a requirement, where a provision, criterion or practice of A's puts a disabled person at a substantial disadvantage in relation to a relevant matter in comparison with persons who are not disabled, to take such steps as it is reasonable to have to take to avoid the disadvantage.

(4) The second requirement is a requirement, where a physical feature puts a disabled person at a substantial disadvantage in relation to a relevant matter in comparison with persons who are not disabled, to take such steps as it is reasonable to have to take to avoid the disadvantage . . .

EA 2010, s. 21

(1) A failure to comply with the first [or] second . . . requirement is a failure to comply with a duty to make reasonable adjustments.

(2) A discriminates against a disabled person if A fails to comply with that duty in relation to that person.

KEY CASE

Archibald v *Fife Council* **[2004] IRLR 651**

Concerning: duty to make reasonable adjustments

Facts

Mrs Archibald was employed as a road sweeper. After a routine surgical procedure she became unable to walk. This meant she could no longer do her job. Mrs Archibald applied for a number of sedentary office-based jobs. However, she was unsuccessful and was dismissed.

Legal principle

The House of Lords held that:

■ the duty to make reasonable adjustments is a positive duty. Unlike discrimination law in the context of the other protected characteristics such as sex, race, sexual orientation, etc., the duty to make reasonable adjustments in favour of disabled persons obliges an employer to positively discriminate in favour of disabled people, i.e. treat them differently – and more favourably – than non-disabled employees where the former have been put at a 'substantial disadvantage';

■ the positive obligation to make reasonable adjustments potentially may include:

  □ allowing disabled people to trump applicants for existing vacancies even where the disabled person is not the best candidate for that vacancy, provided that the disabled person is suitable to do that work; and

  □ creating a new post for the disabled employee, e.g. see *Southampton City College* v *Randall* (2006) and *Chief Constable of South Yorkshire Police* v *Jelic* (2010).

! Don't be tempted to . . .

You should not fall into the trap of thinking that an employer's duty to make reasonable adjustments is restricted to physical features of its premises. In *Nottinghamshire CC* v *Meikle* (2004), the Court of Appeal made it clear that the duty to make reasonable adjustments extended beyond physical features of the workplace to terms, conditions and arrangements of the workplace such as hours of work, duties and contractual sick pay. This is now reflected in section 20(3) and (4) of the EA 2010, which requires the tribunal to consider whether:

(a) any provisions, criteria or practices, or

(b) physical features of the employer's premises, put disabled persons at a 'substantial disadvantage' compared to non-disabled persons.

Requirement for a comparator

In determining whether there is a 'substantial disadvantage', a comparator for the disabled person must be selected. *Smith* v *Churchills Stairlifts plc* (2006) held that the correct comparator is not the population as a whole, but those others who fulfil the other conditions for the job who are not disabled.

The 'reasonableness' test in section 20(1), EA 2010

Two important points can be made in relation to the reasonableness test in section 20(1):

(1) It is an objective test, which is amply demonstrated by *Collins* v *Royal National Theatre Board Ltd* (2004) and the judgment of Kay LJ in *Smith* v *Churchills Stairlifts plc* (2006) at p. 47.

(2) In considering the employer's duty to make reasonable adjustments in a given case, an employer will not be in breach of duty if it merely fails to consider making a proper assessment of the reasonable steps which it ought to take. Instead, the duty to make reasonable adjustments is limited to what an employer did or did not do – not what they had considered – see *Tarbuck* v *Sainsbury's Supermarkets Ltd* (2006).

Once a disabled claimant has established that the application of a provision, criterion or practice, or the physical features of the employer's premises, places him or her at a substantial disadvantage, a tribunal must identify with some particularity what 'step' it is that the employer is said to have failed to take. Unless that is done the kind of assessment of reasonableness required by the EA 2010 is not possible and the employer will not be held to be in breach of the duty to make reasonable adjustments – see *HM Prison Service* v *Johnson* (2007).

Discrimination arising from disability

Discrimination arising from disability is a concept which is peculiar to disability. It has no equivalent counterpart in the context of the other protected characteristics.

KEY STATUTE

EA 2010, s. 15

(1) A person (A) discriminates against a disabled person (B) if –

    (a) A treats B unfavourably because of something arising in consequence of B's disability, and

    (b) A cannot show that the treatment is a proportionate means of achieving a legitimate aim.

(2) Subsection (1) does not apply if A shows that A did not know, and could not reasonably have been expected to know, that B had the disability.

'Unfavourably'

As stated above, section 15 of the EA 2010 replaces a statutory concept known as 'disability-related discrimination', which was set out in section 3A(1) of the DDA 1995. This provided that a disabled person would be discriminated against if, for a reason which related to his or her disability, he or she was treated less favourably than a person to whom the disability-related reason did not or would not apply. Unlike section 15 of the EA 2010, section 3A(1) of the DDA 1995 entailed comparing the disabled person with a comparator and in the key case of *Mayor and Burgesses of the London Borough of Lewisham* v *Malcolm* (2008), the House of Lords held that the comparison focused on the disability itself, rather than the non-disability reason.

KEY CASE

Mayor and Burgesses of the London Borough of Lewisham v *Malcolm* [2008] IRLR 700

Concerning: the appropriate comparator for 'disability-related discrimination' in s. 3A(1) DDA 1995

Facts

Mr Malcolm, a schizophrenic who took medication, occupied local authority housing under a secure tenancy. During a period when he had failed to take his medication, he sub-let his flat to a third party and vacated the property, all in breach of his tenancy agreement. When he reoccupied the property once the sub-let had ended, the local authority commenced proceedings to recover possession. Mr Malcolm claimed that the local authority discriminated against him in seeking to recover possession since the reason he had entered into the sub-let was that he had suffered a serious relapse of his schizophrenic illness. He argued that disability-related discrimination was demonstrated by the fact that, for a reason related to his schizophrenic illness (which is a disability), the local authority had treated him less favourably than others to whom that reason would not apply.

Legal principle

The House of Lords held that:

- section 3A(1)(a) of the DDA 1995 enjoined Mr Malcolm to compare himself with a non-disabled person who had also sub-let his flat to a third party in breach of the non-disabled person's tenancy agreement;

- thus, pursuant to section 3A(1) of the DDA 1995, a disabled person must compare himself with a non-disabled person to whom the disability-related reason also applies – not a disabled or non-disabled person to whom the disability-related reason does not apply.

Since Mr Malcolm had been treated by the local authority in exactly the same way as third parties who had also sub-let would have been treated, the conclusion was that there was no 'disability-related discrimination'.

! Don't be tempted to . . .

You should not fall into the trap of thinking that the case of *Mayor and Burgesses of the London Borough of Lewisham* v *Malcolm* (2008) construes how section 15 of the EA 2010 operates. However, you must understand that there is a direct link between that case and section 15 of the EA 2010. Since the case decided that the disabled person must compare herself or himself with a non-disabled person to whom the reason for the employer's treatment also applied, rather than a disabled or non-disabled person to whom the reason for the employer's treatment did not apply, the effect of this decision was that it was made very difficult for a disabled person to be successful in a claim of disability-related discrimination under section 3A(1) of the DDA 1995. For example, consider a disabled person who is arthritic and cannot type. That person would have to show less favourable treatment by comparing him/herself to a non-disabled person who also could not type. It was more difficult for the arthritic person to show less favourable treatment in terms of that test than if they were required to show less favourable treatment when he/she compared him/herself with a disabled or non-disabled person who could type. The UK Government consulted on the decision in *Mayor and Burgesses of the London Borough of Lewisham* v *Malcolm* (2008) and repealed the concept of 'disability-related discrimination' in the DDA 1995. The Government stated that its intention in introducing the concept of 'discrimination arising from disability' in section 15 of the EA 2010 was to reverse the effect of *Malcolm* and re-establish 'an appropriate balance between enabling a disabled person to make out a case of experiencing a detriment which arises because of his or her disability, and providing an opportunity for an employer . . . to defend the treatment'. Therefore, commentators such as Hepple (2014) expressed the view that the word 'unfavourably' completely removes the need for any comparison exercise between the disabled employee and an actual or hypothetical comparator. This interpretation of section 15 of the EA 2010 was applied by the Supreme Court in *Akerman-Livingstone* v *Aster Communities Ltd* (2015).

Section 15(1)(b) justification

An employer can justify discrimination arising from disability by showing that the unfavourable treatment suffered by a disabled employee was a proportionate means of achieving a legitimate aim. Therefore, the employer has a 'proportionality' defence. As confirmed in *Akerman-Livingstone* v *Aster Communities Ltd* (2015) and *Trustees of Swansea University Pension Scheme* v *Williams* (2015), this defence operates in the same fashion as the proportionality defence in the case of the statutory concept of indirect discrimination (examined in Chapter 5).

Direct discrimination

The definition of direct disability discrimination is contained in section 13(1) and (3) of the EA 2010.

KEY STATUTE

EA 2010, s. 13

(1) A person (A) discriminates against another (B) if, because of a protected characteristic, A treats B less favourably than A treats or would treat others . . .

(3) If the protected characteristic is disability, and B is not a disabled person, A does not discriminate against B only because A treats or would treat disabled persons more favourably than A treats B.

📖 **REVISION NOTE**

Direct discrimination was examined in detail in Chapter 5. Direct disability discrimination follows the same pattern. See Figure 5.1 for an outline.

Indirect discrimination

The definition of indirect disability discrimination is contained in section 19 of the EA 2010.

📖 **REVISION NOTE**

Indirect discrimination was examined in detail in Chapter 5. Indirect disability discrimination follows the same pattern. See Figure 5.2 for an outline.

■ Age discrimination

Age discrimination follows the same pattern as that applicable in the context of other protected characteristics. However, there are some issues that are specific to age discrimination which we will now consider.

Direct discrimination

Section 13(1) and (2) of the EA 2010 make it clear that direct age discrimination may be justified by the employer if it can show that the less favourable treatment was a proportionate means of achieving a legitimate aim. An adjusted flowchart for direct discrimination in the case of age is shown as Figure 6.2.

❗ Don't be tempted to . . .

You should remember that it is possible to justify direct age discrimination and, to that extent, this feature sets the protected characteristic of age apart from the other protected characteristics. The EHRC has provided guidance on the correct approach to the employer's proportionality defence in the case of a claim of direct age discrimination ▶

---

at p. 57 of the Equality Act 2010 Code of Practice on Employment (see http://equalityhumanrights.com/uploaded_files/EqualityAct/employercode.pdf). The EHRC advises that the correct approach is to address the following questions:

■ First, is the aim of the rule or practice legal and non-discriminatory, and one that represents a real, objective consideration?

■ Secondly, if the aim is legitimate, is the means of achieving it proportionate – that is, appropriate and necessary in all the circumstances?

There is no list of aims of the employer which are automatically treated as 'legitimate', but it is suggested that the aims listed in Figure 6.3 provide an indication of what a court or tribunal might find acceptable. Meanwhile, at p. 58 of the Equality Act 2010 Code of Practice on Employment (mentioned above), the EHRC offer up the following example as one where the employer would fail to satisfy the proportionality defence:

Example

A fashion retailer rejects a middle-aged woman as a sales assistant on the grounds that she is 'too old' for the job. They tell her that they need to attract the young customer base at which their clothing is targeted. If this corresponds to a real business need on the part of the retailer, it could qualify as a legitimate aim. However, rejecting this middle-aged woman is unlikely to be a proportionate means of achieving this aim; a requirement for all sales assistants to have knowledge of the products and fashion awareness would be a less discriminatory means of making sure the aim is achieved.

Figure 6.2

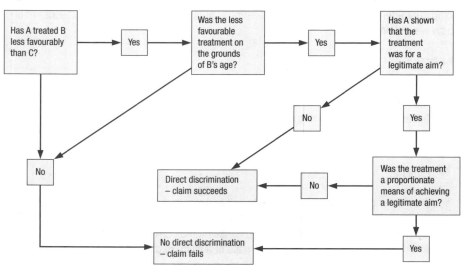

Figure 6.3

Legitimate aims
1 Protection or promotion of vocational integration of a particular age group
2 Health, welfare and safety
3 Particular training requirements
4 Recruiting or retaining older people
5 Encouraging and rewarding loyalty
6 The need for a reasonable period of employment before retirement

■ Putting it all together

Answer guidelines

See the problem question at the start of this chapter. A diagram illustrating how to structure your answer is available on the website.

Approaching the question

The focus in this question is on the steps which it is reasonable for an employer to have to take in order to comply with its duty to make reasonable adjustments under sections 20 to 22 of the EA 2010. See below for further details.

Important points to include

Points to remember when answering this question:

- Explain that the employee may have a claim for breach of the employer's statutory duty to make reasonable adjustments.
- Consider whether the employer has applied a 'provision, criterion or practice'.
- If so, is the employee placed at a 'substantial disadvantage'? How do the tribunals ascertain whether there is 'substantial disadvantage'?
- Examine the reasonable steps or adjustments which the employer might take in the employee's case.

Make your answer stand out

Consider the implications of *Archibald* v *Fife Council* (2004). Do you think it is satisfactory that the duty to make reasonable adjustments involves employers positively discriminating in favour of disabled persons?

READ TO IMPRESS

Connolly, M. (2011) *Discrimination Law*, 2nd edn, London: Sweet & Maxwell, chs 4 and 13.

Hepple, B. (2014) *Equality: The New Legal Framework*, 2nd edn, Oxford: Hart.

www.pearsoned.co.uk/lawexpress

 Go online to access more revision support including quizzes to test your knowledge, sample questions with answer guidelines, podcasts you can download, and more!

Equal pay

Revision checklist

Essential points you should know:

- [ ] The content of the equality clause
- [ ] The distinction between the three criteria of 'like work', 'work rated as equivalent' and 'work of equal value' in section 65 of the Equality Act 2010 (EA 2010)
- [ ] The content of the employer's defence to an equal pay claim based on material factors
- [ ] The relationship between Chapter 3 of Part 5 of the EA 2010 and Article 157 of the Treaty on the Functioning of the European Union (TFEU)

■ Topic map

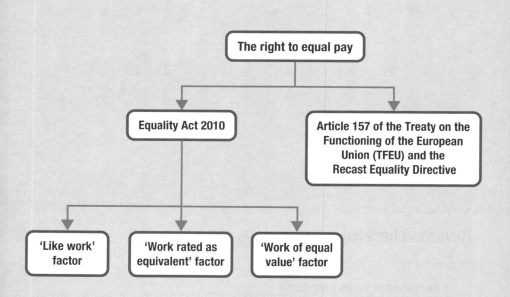

■ Introduction

A female employee is entitled to the same pay as a suitable male employee comparator.

This chapter examines the principle of equal pay for equal work. It examines how a female employee is entitled to the same remuneration as a suitable male employee comparator. The equal pay rules are contained in Chapter 3 of Part 5 of the Equality Act 2010 (EA 2010) and their intention is to eliminate sex discrimination in pay – not to secure 'fair wages'. In terms of section 69 of the EA 2010, an employer has a defence to an equal pay claim. Article 157 of the Treaty on the Functioning of the European Union (TFEU) – which secures equal pay for equal work – must also be considered.

ASSESSMENT ADVICE

Essay questions

These require broad general knowledge of the principles of equal pay in Chapter 3 of Part 5 of the EA 2010 and the exceptions to these principles. Essays may also require you to explore the right of an employee to equal pay under Article 157 of the TFEU and how the rules for establishing an equal pay claim differ under the UK and EU regimes. The means of enforcement of equal pay rights under Chapter 3 of Part 5 of the EA 2010 and Article 157 of the TFEU should be examined, compared and contrasted where this is necessary to answer the essay question. In tackling essay questions, you should always directly answer the question(s) asked and apply the relevant law.

Problem questions

Generally, problem questions will involve an examination of the three differing equal pay criteria under section 65 of the EA 2010. In answering a problem question, candidates may be required to explore whether an employer will have the benefit of the material factor defence in section 69 of the EA 2010. In order to appreciate when this exception/ defence applies, candidates must fully understand the content of this defence and the circumstances in which the courts have held a factor to qualify as a material factor. Problem questions may also steer the candidate towards a discussion of Article 157 of the TFEU. In tackling problem questions, you should always directly answer the question(s) asked and apply the relevant law to the facts at hand.

■ Sample question

Could you answer this question? Below is a typical essay question that could arise on this topic. Guidelines on answering the question are included at the end of the chapter, while a sample problem question and guidance on tackling it can be found on the companion website.

> ### ESSAY QUESTION
>
> Critically evaluate the 'material factor' defence which is open to an employer in terms of section 69 of the EA 2010. Do you believe the legal position is satisfactory?

■ The sex equality clause

Section 66 of the EA 2010 imposes a sex equality clause into the contract of employment of every individual employee. There are three principal components of the sex equality clause.

> **KEY STATUTE**
>
> **EA 2010, s. 66**
>
> (1) If the terms of A's work do not (by whatever means) include a sex equality clause, they are to be treated as including one.
>
> (2) A sex equality clause is a provision that has the following effect –
>
>   (a) if a term of A's is less favourable to A than a corresponding term of B's is to B, A's term is modified so as not to be less favourable.
>
>   (b) If A does not have a term which corresponds to a term of B's that benefits B, A's terms are modified so as to include such a term . . .

> ! Don't be tempted to . . .
>
> Don't be fooled into thinking that the statutory notion of a sex equality clause has no effect on the contract of employment. One must be clear that section 66(1) and (2) of the EA 2010 imposes a contractual term into an employee's contract of employment. Since it is a contractual term, it can be enforced in the courts if it is breached. Section 127 of the EA 2010 also provides for enforcement in the employment tribunals. An employee has six months to present such a complaint to an employment tribunal, but if his/her claim is time-barred in the tribunal, in *Abdulla* v *Birmingham City Council* (2013), it was held that the employee may make a claim in court.

Terms

Section 66 of the EA 2010 specifically prohibits discrimination in contractual terms. Since a female employee's terms of employment are compared with the same contractual terms of a male employee, sums payable under a contract such as bonuses, pension contributions and holiday entitlement are all covered and compared, term by term. If there is a valid equal pay claim, the pay-related terms of the female must be brought into line with the same pay-related terms of the male. This is the case, irrespective of whether some of the other pay-related contractual terms of the female are better than those of the male – see *Hayward* v *Cammell Laird Shipbuilders Ltd (No. 2)* (1988). The word 'pay' has an even broader scope under Article 157 of the TFEU – see *Defrenne* v *Belgium* (1971) (at p. 541).

> ✎ **EXAM TIP**
>
> In an essay question or problem question, look out for any assertion in the question that the employee is entitled to be paid a bonus. You should also look out for any suggestion of an employee receiving pension entitlements or contributions or enhanced redundancy benefits or long-term sickness benefits. These items are covered within the compass of section 66 of the EA 2010 and the word 'pay' in Article 157 of the TFEU.

Do the female or male comparators need to work for the same employer?

The answer is no. Section 79 of the EA 2010 provides that a man and a woman will be treated as employed by the same person if the man is employed by the woman's employer or any associated employer (i) at the same establishment or (ii) at an establishment other than the one at which the woman works and common terms and conditions of employment apply at both establishments (either generally or as between the woman and the man). Where the woman and the man work at different establishments, the requirement is to show common terms and conditions in respect of the two establishments rather than between the man and the woman. Two employers are associated with each other if one of them directly or indirectly controls the other or both are directly or indirectly controlled by a third party. The meaning of 'establishment' is assessed with reference to certain factors, namely whether there is a distinct geographical location that is permanent, whether there is exclusive occupation of premises and whether there is some organisation of people working there. Therefore, where the males and females are not working at the same premises but working across different sites, it will not be straightforward for a comparison exercise to be undertaken in such circumstances. For example, see *Edinburgh City Council* v *Wilkinson* (2012) and *Dumfries and Galloway Council* v *North* (2013).

> ✎ **EXAM TIP**
>
> Look out for problem questions which suggest that a female employee cannot identify an actual male comparator. Here, you must consider whether it is possible for her to compare herself with a hypothetical male comparator. For the purposes of Article ▶

157 of the TFEU and the EA 2010, *Macarthys Ltd* v *Smith* (1980) and *Coloroll Pension Trustees Ltd* v *Russell* (1995) demonstrate that a female employee must choose an actual comparator. However, where the female is seeking to challenge a provision of the EA 2010 on the basis that it is inconsistent with EU law, it is open to her to select a hypothetical male comparator – *Allonby* v *Accrington and Rossendale College* (2004). Moreover, an employee is disentitled from comparing herself with a male successor since in *Walton Centre for Neurology and Neurosurgery NHS Trust* v *Bewley* (2008), the EAT ruled that to permit such a claim would amount to an exercise in speculation about what would have occurred if the claimant had been employed contemporaneously with the successor – similar to that involved in a hypothetical comparator exercise.

☐ REVISION NOTE

The issue of an employee's pay is also conditioned by the common law right of employees to be paid if they are ready and willing to work. Statutory provisions such as the National Minimum Wage Act 1998 and Part II of the Employment Rights Act 1996 on the unauthorised deduction of wages should also be borne in mind.

■ 'Like work'

Section 65(1)(a) of the EA 2010 defines one of the components of the sex equality clause. The sex equality clause operates when a woman is employed on 'like work' with a man in the same employment. For the purposes of determining whether a man and woman are employed on 'like work', section 65(2) provides that their work must be the same or broadly similar. Work will be 'broadly similar' if the differences between their work are of no practical importance in relation to the terms of their work. Moreover, the nature, extent and frequency of the differences must be taken into account.

KEY CASE

Capper Pass Ltd v *Lawton* [1976] IRLR 366

Concerning: 'like work'

Facts

A female employee worked as a cook 40 hours a week unsupervised. She prepared and served lunches for between 10 and 20 persons. An assistant chef supervised by a head chef worked 45 hours per week in the canteen and prepared 350 meals a day. It was agreed that the female and male were not engaged in like work, but was their work 'broadly similar'?

> **Legal principle**
>
> It was held that the differences in work between the cook and the assistant chef were of no practical importance and that the work was broadly similar. Accordingly, the 'like work' test in section 1(2)(a) of the Equal Pay Act 1970 (EPA 1970) (the statutory predecessor of section 65(1)(a) of the EA 2010) had been satisfied.

■ 'Work rated as equivalent'

Section 65(1)(b) of the EA 2010 sets out the second component of the sex equality clause. The sex equality clause will operate when a woman is employed on work rated as equivalent with that of a man in the same employment. Here, the jobs of the man and the woman are clearly different. Section 65(2) provides that the work of a woman and a man will be rated as equivalent if their jobs have been given an equal value in terms of demand (based on the criteria of effort, skill and decision making) as part of a voluntary, impartial and suitably analytical job evaluation scheme. An employer is not compelled to produce such a study.

KEY CASE

Springboard Sunderland Trust v *Robson* [1992] IRLR 261

Concerning: 'work rated as equivalent'

Facts

A female employee worked as a team leader and sought to compare herself with a male induction officer. She scored 410 points (after her appeal from 400 points was upheld). The male induction officer scored 428 points. Grade 3 was banded as 360–409 points and grade 4 as 410–449 points. The question was whether their jobs were rated as equivalent.

Legal principle

She was entitled to compare herself with the male induction officer. This was on the basis that their work was rated as equivalent. She was allocated within the same grade as the male. Hence, the differences in the scores were not significant.

KEY CASE

Redcar & Cleveland Borough Council v *Bainbridge* [2007] IRLR 984

Concerning: 'work rated as equivalent'

Facts

This case was brought as a test case forming part of a wider litigation. The question raised was whether it was possible under the EPA 1970 for a claimant to compare ▶

herself with a higher-paid man if her job is graded with a higher value under a job evaluation study.

Legal principle

The Court of Appeal ruled that this question ought to be answered in the affirmative. This involved adding certain words to section 1(5) of the EPA 1970 so that it should read:

A woman is to be regarded as employed on work rated as equivalent with that of any men if, but only if, her job and their job have been given an equal value or her job has been given a higher value, in terms of the demand made on a worker under various headings (for instance effort, skill, decision), on a study undertaken with a view to evaluating in those terms the jobs to be done by all or any of the employees in an undertaking or group of undertakings, or would have been given an equal value, or her job would have been given a higher value, but for the evaluation being made on a system setting different values for men and women on the same demand under any heading.

Murphy v *An Bord Telecom Eirann* (1988) is a similar case.

■ 'Work of equal value'

The third component of the sex equality clause is outlined in section 65(1)(c) of the EA 2010. The equality clause will operate when a woman is employed on work of equal value (based on factors such as effort, skill and decision making) with that of a man in the same employment.

The relationship between 'work of equal value' and 'work rated as equivalent'

The 'work of equal value' component was introduced in 1983 by the UK Government. It was introduced to comply with the predecessor of what is now Article 157 of the TFEU, since under the pre-1983 law there was no mechanism other than the 'work rated as equivalent' criterion to enable a female employee to compare herself with a male employee doing a different job. Since the job evaluation scheme, which forms the basis of the 'work rated as equivalent' test, is (and was) purely voluntary there was no basis on which a female employee could force an employer to grade different jobs in terms of demands such as effort, skill and decision making. Section 65(1)(c) of the EA 2010 fills the gap by enabling a female employee who believes that her work is of equal value with that of a man doing a different job to ascertain the validity of her claim. An employment tribunal has the power to select and appoint an independent expert to carry out a job evaluation study in terms of section 131 of the EA 2010.

■ Material factor defence

Once a female employee has:

■ identified a suitable male comparator;

■ demonstrated that one of her terms is less generous than his;

■ demonstrated that one of the 'like work', 'work rated as equivalent' or 'work of equal value' tests has been satisfied,

a rebuttable presumption of unequal terms/pay or sex discrimination in terms/pay arises. The onus then falls on the employer to rebut that presumption. This is achieved by demonstrating that the pay differential is genuinely due to a material factor which is completely gender neutral: section 69 of the EA 2010.

Material factors

Case law has established a number of material factors which are gender neutral (see Figure 7.1).

Figure 7.1

Case name	Legal principle
Cadman [2006] IRLR 969	Rebuttable presumption that length of service is a material factor
Jørgensen [2000] IRLR 726	Budgetary constraints cannot be a material factor
Rainey [1987] IRLR 26	Rebuttable presumption that market forces are material factors
Enderby [1993] IRLR 591	Where collective agreement results in pay disparities, this is unlikely to be a material factor

What if the material factor is not gender neutral?

If the female employee can provide evidence that the material factor is not gender neutral but that it in fact functions in a way which is discriminatory or exhibits a direct or indirect discriminatory impact, then the onus reverts to the employer to justify objectively (pursuant to the proportionality test we considered in Chapters 5 and 6) the difference in the terms of the female and of the male employee (see Figure 7.2). This is the position in the domestic courts under the EA 2010 (*Glasgow City Council* v *Marshall* (2000), *Villalba* v *Merrill Lynch & Co. Inc* (2006) and *Armstrong* v *Newcastle upon Tyne NHS Hospital Trust* (2006)).

Figure 7.2

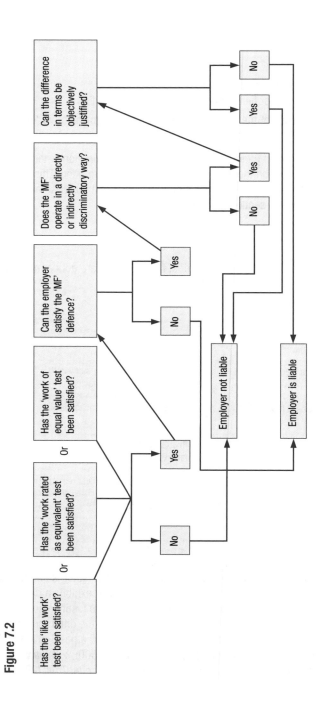

Make your answer stand out

Students who are able to demonstrate in their exam answers that the current domestic position is arguably inconsistent with EU law jurisprudence are likely to gain extra marks: see *Brunnhofer* v *Bank der Österreichischen Postsparkasse AG* (2001) and *Sharp* v *Caledonia Group Services Ltd* (2006). EU jurisprudence requires an employer to justify objectively whether a material factor resulting in a pay disparity is gender neutral or not.

■ Article 157 of the TFEU and the Recast Equality Directive

Article 157 of the TFEU must also be considered. It imposes an obligation on the UK and other member states to ensure that the principle of equal pay for male and female workers for equal work or work of equal value applies. While Article 157 may be used in domestic courts to interpret domestic law which is inconsistent with EU law, it confers no separate free-standing right. The Recast Equality Directive is directly effective against emanations of the state. Meanwhile, Article 157 is directly effective against public or private employers. If any provision of the EA 2010 is incompatible with EU law, the claimant is entitled to rely directly on the EU provisions and case law and to argue that the incompatible domestic provision should be disapplied.

! **Don't be tempted to . . .**

Take care not to assume that a female employee will invariably be able to compare herself with a male employee working for the same employer as a general rule in an equal pay claim. There are circumstances when a claim must fail even where the female and male have the same employer. For example, in *Lawrence* v *Regent Office Care Ltd* (2002), the ECJ held that where differences in pay or conditions cannot be attributed to a single source, there is no body which is responsible for the inequality and which could restore equal treatment. Therefore, such a situation does not come within the compass of Article 157. In *Robertson* v *DEFRA* (2005), the 'single source' test was applied to prevent female civil servants in one Government department from comparing themselves with male civil servants in another Government department – even though they had the same employer, i.e. the Crown. The Court of Appeal came to the same conclusion that a female employee could not compare herself with a male employee – where they both had the same employer in the case of *Armstrong* v *Newcastle upon Tyne NHS Hospital Trust* (2006). Here the equal pay claim of a female employee ▶

working for an NHS Trust failed under Article 157 on the basis of the absence of a 'single source'. She had attempted to compare herself with a male employee working for the same NHS Trust at a different hospital (although they had originally worked for two different NHS Trusts, which had then merged).

▉ Putting it all together

Answer guidelines

See the essay question at the start of this chapter. A diagram illustrating how to structure your answer is available on the website.

Approaching the question

The focus in this question is on the material factor defence of the employer where a rebuttable presumption of unequal pay or sex discrimination in contractual terms/pay arises. See below for further details.

Important points to include

Points to remember when answering this question:

- Clarify that Chapter 3 of Part 5 of the EA 2010 is about the contractual terms of men and women doing 'like work', 'work rated as equivalent' or 'work of equal value' being different.
- An exploration of the key concepts of 'like work', 'work rated as equivalent' or 'work of equal value' is essential.
- Include a discussion centred on criteria which qualify as 'material factors'.
- Examine the relationship and differences between the regimes under Chapter 3 of Part 5 of the EA 2010 and Article 157 of the TFEU, i.e. the difference in the stages at which objective justification must take place – see Figure 7.2 above.

 Make your answer stand out

Consider whether domestic law conforms with the 'single source' test in EU law and whether UK law is in breach of EU law in failing to compel an employer to justify objectively at an earlier stage in the 'material factor' process – see Figure 7.2.

READ TO IMPRESS

Barrett, G. (2006) 'Shall I compare thee to . . .?': on Article 141 EC and *Lawrence*. 35 *Industrial Law Journal*: 93.

Connolly, M. (2011) *Discrimination Law*, 2nd edn, London: Sweet & Maxwell, ch. 9.

Freedman, S. (2008) Reforming equal pay laws. 37 *Industrial Law Journal*: 193.

Hepple, B. (2014) *Equality: The New Legal Framework*, 2nd edn, Oxford: Hart, 105–134.

Rowbottom, D. (2010) Justifying service-related pay in the context of sex discrimination law. 39 *Industrial Law Journal*: 382.

Steele, I. (2008) Beyond equal pay. 37 *Industrial Law Journal*: 119.

Steele, I. (2010) Sex discrimination and the material factor defence under the Equal Pay Act 1970 and the Equality Act 2010. 39 *Industrial Law Journal*: 264.

www.pearsoned.co.uk/lawexpress

Go online to access more revision support including quizzes to test your knowledge, sample questions with answer guidelines, podcasts you can download, and more!

Wrongful
dismissal

Revision checklist

Essential points you should know:

- [ ] When a dismissal will be wrongful
- [ ] How wrongful dismissal claims are enforced
- [ ] The difference between wrongful dismissal and unfair dismissal
- [ ] What can and cannot be compensated under a wrongful dismissal claim

◼ Topic map

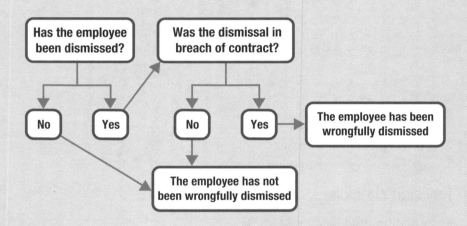

■ Introduction

An employee has a common law right not to be wrongfully dismissed.

This chapter examines the concept of wrongful dismissal which exists at common law. It analyses when a dismissed employee will be entitled to raise a wrongful dismissal claim. An employee will be deemed to have been wrongfully dismissed when:

1. the employee has been dismissed (actually or constructively);
2. the dismissal was a repudiatory breach of contract on the part of the employer.

A common example is where an employee is dismissed without notice or with less notice than he/she is contractually entitled to receive.

ASSESSMENT ADVICE

Essay questions

These require broad general knowledge of the principles of wrongful dismissal and how such claims are enforced. You will also be expected to know the difference between a wrongful dismissal claim and a claim for unfair dismissal (see Chapter 9). The key difference is that a wrongful dismissal claim exists at *common law* only and is usually enforced in the courts, whereas an unfair dismissal claim is a *statutory claim* which can only be enforced in an employment tribunal. See Figure 8.1 for the other differences between the two claims. A number of cases have explored the losses which may be compensated under a claim of wrongful dismissal. Essay questions may require you to deal with these issues in some detail.

Problem questions

These may involve an examination of the facts with a view to determining whether an individual who has been dismissed has a reasonable prospect of success in pursuing a wrongful dismissal claim, i.e. that an employee has been dismissed (or constructively dismissed) in breach of contract. The problem question may also list a number of losses sustained by the dismissed individual. You may be required to analyse whether the law permits the individual to be compensated in respect of such losses.

■ Sample question

Could you answer this question? Below is a typical problem question that could arise on this topic. Guidelines on answering the question are included at the end of the chapter, while a sample essay question and guidance on tackling it can be found on the companion website.

PROBLEM QUESTION

Hugh has worked for Offdesk plc for one year and 10 months as a senior bond trader. His contract of employment states that his employer must give him four months' prior notice of dismissal and he is entitled to be paid a guaranteed bonus so long as he is employed at the bonus payment date – which is only five weeks away. Hugh is Mary's line manager. A serious allegation is made against him by Mary. Hugh's employer's reaction is immediately to suspend him. No investigation into the allegations is undertaken. Six days after the making of the allegation Hugh is summoned to a meeting with the human resources director and chairman of the employer. The human resources director verbally abuses him in front of the chairman and calls him 'completely useless and incompetent from day one'. The chairman explains that the employer believes that the allegations made by Mary are 'a pack of lies'. However, they have nonetheless decided to dismiss Hugh and hand him a letter. He is asked to clear his desk and immediately remove himself from the premises. Outside the building, Hugh notes that the letter includes a cheque made payable to him. It explains that the cheque comprises his wages to the date of dismissal (i.e. that very day) and that the reason for his dismissal is incompetence. As a result of the whole sorry experience, Hugh suffers a psychiatric injury. Advise Hugh.

◾ The meaning of 'wrongful dismissal'

An employee is wrongfully dismissed when he or she is dismissed by his or her employer in breach of his or her contract of employment. A **wrongful dismissal** most commonly occurs where an employee is dismissed without notice or with less notice than the employee is entitled to receive. Another situation where an employee may be held to have been wrongfully dismissed is where he or she is working on the basis of a **fixed-term contract** and it is terminated before the expiry date. The key thing to consider is whether:

- the employee has been dismissed;
- the dismissal was in **repudiatory breach of contract** on the part of the employer.

KEY DEFINITION: Wrongful dismissal

A dismissal of an employee which amounts to a repudiatory breach of contract on the part of the employer.

For an example of wrongful dismissal, see *McClelland* v *Northern Ireland General Health Services Board* (1957).

> **KEY DEFINITION: Fixed-term contract**
>
> A contract which endures for a specific period of time and terminates at the end of that period of time.

> **KEY DEFINITION: Repudiatory breach of contract**
>
> A breach of a term of a contract which goes to the root of that contract so that on the occurrence of breach the innocent party may be regarded as discharged from further performance of his or her obligations under the contract.

> 📖 **REVISION NOTE**
>
> In Chapter 4, we explored the minimum periods of notice of termination which an employee is entitled to receive from an employer. These minimum periods of notice are based on statute (s. 86(1) of the Employment Rights Act 1996 (ERA 1996)). If the period of the employee's continuous employment with the employer is less than two years, the employee is entitled to one week's notice. Thereafter, he or she is entitled to an extra week's notice for every extra year he or she has been continuously employed by his or her employer. This is subject to a maximum limit of 12 weeks' notice. The terms of the employee's written contract of employment may increase the period of notice.

■ The enforcement of wrongful dismissal claims

Claims for wrongful dismissal are essentially common law claims. Hence, they are enforceable in the courts. However, in terms of section 3 of the ERA 1996, the Employment Tribunals Extension of Jurisdiction (England and Wales) Order 1994 and the Employment Tribunals Extension of Jurisdiction (Scotland) Order 1994, wrongful dismissal claims may also be enforced in the employment tribunals. Enforcing a wrongful dismissal claim in an employment tribunal, however, will not always be an attractive route for an employee since compensation is capped at a maximum of £25,000 per claim.

■ The difference between 'wrongful dismissal' claims and unfair dismissal complaints

When an employee has been dismissed, his or her legal advisers will need to decide whether:

- to raise a wrongful dismissal claim in the courts or employment tribunal; or
- to present a complaint to an employment tribunal for unfair dismissal, which Part X of the ERA 1996 states can only be enforced in an employment tribunal.

📖 **REVISION NOTE**

In Chapter 10, we discuss the ACAS Code of Practice on Disciplinary and Grievance Procedures which an employer must comply with prior to dismissing an employee in terms of section 207A of, and Sched. A2 to, the Trade Union and Labour Relations (Consolidation) Act 1992. If an employee enforces his wrongful dismissal claim in the employment tribunal, the employee's award of damages may be increased by up to 25 per cent if the employer has failed to follow the ACAS Code of Practice.

✎ **EXAM TIP**

There are many differences between a common law claim for wrongful dismissal and a statutory claim for unfair dismissal. Where an employee is dismissed, he or she may have the option of presenting both a wrongful dismissal and an unfair dismissal claim and will be required to choose between them. An employee who has been dismissed must choose whether to raise proceedings based on one or the other. Figure 8.1 outlines the differences between the two and can be used to decide which proceedings to raise.

Figure 8.1

Unfair dismissal	Wrongful dismissal
1. Statutory right	1. Common law right
2. Enforced in employment tribunals	2. Enforced in courts and can only be enforced in tribunal if claim is less than £25,000
3. Maximum limit on compensation (currently £93,332)	3. Unlimited compensation
4. Individual must be an employee	4. Not essential that individual is an employee
5. Individual must have been continuously employed for at least two years	5. No prerequisite of a minimum length of service
6. Individuals employed in certain industry sectors or trades are excluded from the right not to be unfairly dismissed	6. No exclusions from right based on industry sectors or trades
7. Individual can claim unfair dismissal even though he has been dismissed with due notice of termination or a fixed-term contract has expired without renewal	7. It is not possible to claim wrongful dismissal where an employee has been given due notice or a fixed-term contract has expired without renewal

📖 REVISION NOTE

The topic of wrongful dismissal overlaps with unfair dismissal. You should not consider these topics separately but in tandem.

■ What can and cannot be compensated under a wrongful dismissal claim

Where an employee suffers monetary or non-monetary losses as a result of being wrongfully dismissed, the employee can claim compensation from his or her employer in respect of the following:

- losses suffered where the employee (i) has been dismissed without the period of notice of termination to which he or she is legally entitled and (ii) has not received payment in lieu of notice. For example, if an employee is entitled to four weeks' notice of termination and does not receive this, the employee should receive four weeks' pay in lieu. If he or she does not, then he or she will be entitled to four weeks' pay in compensation pursuant to her wrongful dismissal claim;
- contractual benefits which the employee would have been entitled to receive during his or her notice period, e.g. if the period of notice which he or she is entitled to receive is four weeks, then he or she is entitled to be compensated for four weeks' worth of contractual benefits, such as pension benefits, bonus payments, sickness insurance payments and use of company car, etc.;
- 'stigma' damages, i.e. losses which the employee has suffered as a result of his or her inability to obtain alternative employment in the labour market as a result of the stigma associated with the dishonest or fraudulent practices of his or her former employer;
- losses suffered as a result of events leading up to the dismissal which are in breach of contract, e.g. a breach of an implied term or express term of the contract of employment.

However, an employee is barred from obtaining damages in respect of losses occasioned by an employer's failure to comply with a contractually agreed disciplinary process: *Edwards* v *Chesterfield Royal Hospital NHS Foundation Trust* (2012). In such a case, the employee's remedy will be restricted to an injunction preventing the employer's non-adherence to the disciplinary procedure.

The main head of loss which employees may sustain is the failure of the employer to pay them in lieu of notice. In other words, where an employer dismisses an employee without (i) permitting him or her to work out his or her notice period of four weeks and (ii) paying him or her four weeks' pay in lieu of notice, that employee will have a claim for four weeks' notice pay in respect of the four-week period of notice to which he or she was entitled. The case of *Addis* v *Gramophone Co. Ltd* (1909) is a classic example. The House of Lords held in *Addis* that an employee could only claim damages for arrears of notice pay and other financial losses accruing during the notice period where he or she had been wrongfully dismissed.

Lost wages and contractual benefits

Together with arrears of notice pay, an employee may seek damages in respect of wages and other contractual benefits (such as pension benefits, bonus payments and sickness insurance payments) which he or she is entitled to receive, but which have not been paid or received. The measure of damages will be a sum equivalent to the wages and contractual benefits which would have been earned, between the time of actual termination and the time which the contract might lawfully have been terminated (by due notice).

'Stigma' damages and injury to feelings

The case of *Addis* v *Gramophone Co. Ltd* (1909) represents a bar to an employee claiming damages in respect of injury to feelings and mental distress which he or she has suffered as a result of a wrongful dismissal. In addition, *Addis* held that an employee could not claim damages in respect of the difficulties which he or she might have experienced in gaining alternative employment on the labour market. The case of *Malik* v *BCCI SA (in liquidation)* (1997) altered the position in respect of the latter issue. Hence, the law now permits employees to claim compensation for 'stigma' damages.

KEY CASE

Malik v *BCCI SA (in liquidation)* [1997] IRLR 462

Concerning: 'stigma' damages, breach of implied term of mutual trust and confidence

Facts

An employee who previously worked for BCCI could not obtain alternative employment in the labour market because of the 'stigma' associated with his having worked previously for BCCI. BCCI had engaged in fraudulent transactions and practices.

Legal principle

Overturning the principle in *Addis* v *Gramophone Co. Ltd* (1909), it was held that an employee could be compensated in respect of 'stigma' damages. However, the principle in *Addis* that injury to feelings and mental distress which an employee has suffered cannot be compensated still stands as good law.

📖 REVISION NOTE

The issue of 'stigma' damages is relevant to the discussion of the implied term of mutual trust and confidence in Chapters 2 and 3 (see key definition in Chapter 2). An employee may allege that he or she is entitled to compensation for 'stigma' damages. This is on the basis that the employer breached the implied term of mutual trust and confidence in running a fraudulent, corrupt and dishonest business.

The act of dismissal and events leading up to it

The cases of *Johnson* v *Unisys Ltd* (2001) and *Eastwood* v *Magnox Electric plc* (2004) decided that where the act of, or manner of, the dismissal of an employee breaches an implied term (e.g. the implied term of mutual trust and confidence (see Chapters 2 and 3)) of the contract of employment, compensation is barred. For example, if an employer shouts or swears at and/or humiliates an employee when the employee is dismissed and the employee suffers a psychiatric injury as a result, the employee will not be entitled to compensation as a result of this breach of the implied term of mutual trust and confidence. The reason the House of Lords gave for this in *Johnson* is that to award compensation in such circumstances would circumvent the intention of Parliament in introducing limited compensation for dismissal under the unfair dismissal regime in Part X of the ERA 1996.

However, where events leading up to the dismissal (e.g. the suspension of the employee, investigations regarding allegations made against the employee or the disciplinary hearing of the employee) are conducted by the employer in a manner which amounts to a breach of an implied term (e.g. the implied term of mutual trust and confidence) of the contract of employment and the employee suffers loss as a result, the employee may be compensated in respect of such losses.

📖 REVISION NOTE

The issue of compensation for events leading up to a dismissal depends on whether there has been a breach of the contract of employment. For these purposes, the implied term of mutual trust and confidence, which was considered in Chapters 2 and 3, is important – since a breach of the implied term by the employer will amount to a breach of contract.

✎ EXAM TIP

In a problem question which asks you to consider whether compensation is available to an employee in relation to his or her dismissal, students should divide the series of factual events into:

(a)   the act of dismissal itself;

(b)   the events leading up to the dismissal (e.g. the act of suspension, the disciplinary investigation, the disciplinary hearing, the disciplinary appeal hearing and the appeal hearing).

If (a) has been conducted in breach of contract, no compensation is available to an employee. However, if any of (b) are undertaken in breach of contract, damages may be claimed by an employee.

Recovery of compensation for loss of opportunity to claim unfair dismissal

In order to qualify for the unfair dismissal right under section 94(1) of the ERA 1996, an employee must have been continuously employed with his or her employer for at least two years. If the employer deliberately dismisses the employee prior to the two-year threshold, can an employee claim compensation from the employer in respect of the loss of opportunity to bring a claim for unfair dismissal under the bracket of a wrongful dismissal claim? See *Virgin Net Ltd* v *Harper* (2004).

KEY CASE

Virgin Net Ltd v *Harper* [2004] IRLR 390

Concerning: loss of opportunity to claim unfair dismissal

Facts

Miss Harper's contract of employment provided that she was entitled to three months' notice of termination. She was dismissed without receiving notice of termination 33 days short of the date when she would have completed the one-year period of employment qualifying her to bring a claim of unfair dismissal. She raised a wrongful dismissal claim and sought compensation for the loss of the opportunity to claim unfair dismissal.

Legal principle

The Court of Appeal held that Miss Harper was not entitled to be compensated in respect of the loss of opportunity to claim unfair dismissal. In fact, the Court of Appeal went so far as to say that she had not lost the right to claim compensation for unfair dismissal by being dismissed without her contractual notice. She never had such a right in the first place because she fell short of the requirement of one year's continuous service which Parliament had prescribed. The length of service requirement is now two years.

Recovery of compensation for contractually guaranteed payments

Where an employee's contract of employment provides that the employee is entitled to a 'guaranteed' bonus payment (or some other form of remuneration) and he or she is dismissed by the employer as a means of avoiding the payment of such bonus, this will amount to a breach of an implied term of the contract of employment. As a result, the employee may recover compensation. An 'anti-avoidance' implied term of the contract of employment appears to be emerging. Thus, an employer is under an implied duty not to terminate the employment of an employee in order to avoid the operation of an express term which sanctions the making of certain or conditional payments to the employee. See *Jenvey* v *Australian Broadcasting Corporation* (2002).

Make your answer stand out

The rule in *Johnson* v *Unisys Ltd* (2001) and *Eastwood* v *Magnox Electric plc* (2004) that an employee cannot recover compensation in respect of the act of, or the manner of, the dismissal has caused a lot controversy. The principal reason which Lords Nicholls, Hoffmann and Millett in the House of Lords in *Johnson* and *Eastwood* invoked for their decision not to extend the law is that it would ultimately operate in a way to circumvent the statutory unfair dismissal regime in Part X of the ERA 1996 – which imposes a maximum statutory limit on compensation. In order to attract additional marks in an essay question which asks you about these cases, you should consider whether you agree with the position adopted by Lords Nicholls, Hoffmann and Millett. The articles by Barmes (2004) and Collins and Freedland (2001) and the chapter by Bogg and Collins (2014) will assist you in forming your own opinion.

■ Putting it all together

Answer guidelines

See the problem question at the start of this chapter. A diagram illustrating how to structure your answer is available on the website.

Approaching the question

In order to answer this question properly, you are required to describe and analyse the five distinctive categories of loss in respect of which Hugh may or may not be compensated. It is crucial that you deal with each in turn in your answer. See below for further details.

Important points to include

Points to remember when answering this question:

- Your introduction should provide that the employee has a claim for wrongful dismissal and you should then go on to consider the losses in respect of which compensation may be sought.
- First, the employee will have a claim for four months' pay – Hugh was dismissed without working out his four months' notice period, and was not offered four months' payment in lieu of notice, which amounts to a breach of the contract of employment.
- The employee was dismissed before the two-year qualifying period for unfair dismissal. Consider whether he can claim compensation in respect of the loss of the opportunity to claim unfair dismissal. ▶

- Analyse whether the employee can claim compensation in respect of psychiatric injury caused by (i) the events leading up to the dismissal and/or (ii) the manner of the dismissal.
- Consider the position in respect of the employee's lost bonus entitlement.

 Make your answer stand out

Consider the implications of *Johnson* v *Unisys Ltd* (2001) and *Eastwood* v *Magnox Electric plc* (2004). Is it satisfactory that the employee may claim damages for psychiatric injury caused by the events leading up to the dismissal, but not for the actual dismissal itself or the manner of that dismissal?

READ TO IMPRESS

Barmes, L. (2004) The continuing conceptual crisis in the common law of the contract of employment. 67 *Modern Law Review*: 435.

Barmes, L. (2013) Judicial influence and *Edwards* v *Chesterfield Royal Hospital NHS Trust & Botham* v *Ministry of Defence*. 42 *Industrial Law Journal*: 192.

Barnard, C. (2006) Cherries: one bite or two? 65 *Cambridge Law Journal*: 27.

Barnard, C. and Merrett, L. (2013) Winners and losers: *Edwards* and the unfair law of dismissal. 72 *Cambridge Law Journal*: 313.

Bogg, A. and Collins, H. (2014) Lord Hoffmann and the law of employment: the notorious episode of *Johnson* v *Unisys Ltd*. in Davies, P. S. and Pila, J. (eds), *The Jurisprudence of Lord Hoffmann*, Oxford: Oxford University Press, 185.

Brodie, D. (2001) Mutual trust and the values of the employment contract. 30 *Industrial Law Journal*: 84.

Collins, H. and Freedland, M. (2001) Claim for unfair dismissal. 30 *Industrial Law Journal*: 305.

Ewing, K. (1993) Remedies for breach of the contract of employment. 52 *Cambridge Law Journal*: 405.

McMullen, J. (1997) Extending remedies for breach of the contract of employment. 26 *Industrial Law Journal*: 245.

Reynolds, F. (2010) Non-compliances with a prescribed disciplinary procedure: do ordinary contractual principles apply? 39 *Industrial Law Journal*: 420.

www.pearsoned.co.uk/lawexpress

 Go online to access more revision support including quizzes to test your knowledge, sample questions with answer guidelines, podcasts you can download, and more!

Unfair dismissal (1): basic concepts

Revision checklist

Essential points you should know:

- [ ] The qualifying criteria for an unfair dismissal claim
- [ ] The automatically unfair dismissals
- [ ] The method of enforcement of unfair dismissal claims
- [ ] The three definitions of dismissal in section 95(1) of the Employment Rights Act 1996 (ERA 1996)
- [ ] The five valid reasons for dismissal in section 98(1) and (2) of the ERA 1996
- [ ] How the 'range of reasonable responses' test operates in practice
- [ ] The importance of fair and proper disciplinary procedures and policies

■ Topic map

```
                    ┌─────────────────────┐
                    │  Has the employee   │
          ┌─────────│  been dismissed?    │─────────┐
          │         └─────────────────────┘         │
       ┌──▼──┐                                    ┌──▼──┐
       │ Yes │                                    │ No  │
       └──┬──┘                                    └──┬──┘
          │                                          │
┌─────────▼─────────┐                     ┌──────────▼────────┐
│ Is the applicant  │                     │ Unfair dismissal  │
│ qualified to      │                     │ claim fails       │
│ make a claim?     │                     └───────────────────┘
└─────────┬─────────┘
          │                                          
       ┌──▼──┐                                    ┌─────┐
       │ Yes │                                    │ No  │
       └──┬──┘                                    └──┬──┘
          │                                          │
┌─────────▼─────────┐                     ┌──────────▼────────┐
│ Was the employee  │                     │ Unfair dismissal  │
│ dismissed in      │─────────────────────│ claim fails       │
│ terms of s. 95(1) │                     └───────────────────┘
│ ERA?              │
└─────────┬─────────┘
       ┌──▼──┐
       │ Yes │
       └──┬──┘
          │
┌─────────▼─────────┐
│ Was the employer's│
│ reason for        │
│ dismissal one of  │────────────┐
│ the five          │            │
│ potentially fair  │            │
│ reasons for       │            │
│ dismissal?        │            │
└─────────┬─────────┘            │
       ┌──▼──┐                ┌──▼──┐
       │ Yes │                │ No  │
       └──┬──┘                └──┬──┘
          │                      │
┌─────────▼─────────┐            │
│ Did the employer's│            │
│ decision to       │────────────┤
│ dismiss fall      │            │
│ within the range  │            │
│ of reasonable     │            │
│ responses?        │            │
└─────────┬─────────┘            │
       ┌──▼──┐                   │
       │ Yes │                   │
       └──┬──┘                   │
          │                      │
┌─────────▼─────────┐  ┌─────┐   │  ┌──────────────────┐
│ Did the employer  │  │ No  │───┼─▶│ Claim of unfair  │
│ apply fair and    │─▶└─────┘   │  │ dismissal is     │
│ proper procedures?│            └─▶│ successful       │
└─────────┬─────────┘               │ – order of       │
          │                         │ reinstatement    │
       ┌──▼──┐  ┌──────────────┐    │ or re-engagement │
       │ Yes │─▶│ Unfair       │    │ or compensation  │
       └─────┘  │ dismissal    │    └──────────────────┘
                │ claim fails  │
                └──────────────┘
```

A printable version of this topic map is available from **www.pearsoned.co.uk/lawexpress**

■ Introduction

An employee has a statutory right not to be unfairly dismissed.

This chapter examines the right of an employee not to be unfairly dismissed. It analyses the circumstances when a dismissed employee will have a reasonable prospect of success in asserting his or her statutory right not to be unfairly dismissed. The processes which require to be followed in terms of Part X of the Employment Rights Act 1996 (ERA 1996) in order to determine whether a dismissal is prima facie fair or unfair will be examined. Finally, we will consider the proper and fair disciplinary procedures and policies which an employer must follow prior to the dismissal of an employee.

ASSESSMENT ADVICE

Essay questions

These require broad general knowledge of the principles of unfair dismissal and how such claims are enforced. You will also be expected to know the qualifying criteria for a claim for unfair dismissal and have an understanding of the automatically unfair dismissals (see section 98(3) of the ERA 1996). The statutory definition of 'dismissal' must also be understood, together with the five statutory reasons for dismissal. An appreciation of the 'range of reasonable responses' test is also crucial and demonstrates that you understand how courts and tribunals come to a view as to whether a dismissal is prima facie fair or unfair. The importance of fair and proper disciplinary procedures must also be understood and explored.

Problem questions

These may involve the examination of a particular individual employee's or employer's factual situation with a view to determining whether an individual who has been dismissed has a reasonable prospect of success in pursuing an unfair dismissal claim in an employment tribunal. In answering the problem question, you will need to keep in mind (i) the qualifying criteria for an unfair dismissal claim and (ii) the automatically unfair dismissals. You should also be able to assess whether the facts amount to a 'dismissal' and whether the reason for dismissal is one of the five statutory reasons for dismissal. In coming to a view as to whether a dismissal is prima facie fair or unfair, problem questions may require you to (i) explain and apply the 'range of reasonable responses' test and (ii) assess whether the procedures applied by the employer were fair and proper.

■ Sample question

Could you answer this question? Below is a typical essay question that could arise on this topic. Guidelines on answering the question are included at the end of the chapter, while a sample problem question and guidance on tackling it can be found on the companion website.

> **ESSAY QUESTION**
>
> Evaluate how the 'range of reasonable responses' test is applied in practice. Explain whether you believe this test is a 'perversity' test.

■ The qualifying criteria for unfair dismissal

In order to be eligible to present a complaint of **unfair dismissal** to an employment tribunal, an individual must:

- be an employee;
- have been continuously employed for two years or more (section 108(1) of the ERA 1996);
- not be employed in the police service or the armed forces.

> **KEY DEFINITION: Unfair dismissal**
>
> The dismissal of an employee that is unfair in terms of Part X of the ERA 1996.

> ✎ **EXAM TIP**
>
> In a problem question which concerns an employee who has been dismissed, you must ensure that each of the above four qualifying criteria have been satisfied. Otherwise, the dismissed employee will not be entitled to bring a claim for unfair dismissal. If you are not told so, you should not assume that the employee's length of service is more or less than two years.

■ Enforcement of unfair dismissal claims

Section 111(1) of the ERA 1996 provides that unfair dismissal claims are to be enforced in the employment tribunals.

ERA 1996, s. 111(1)

A complaint may be presented to an employment tribunal against an employer by any person that he was unfairly dismissed by the employer.

Hence, an employee is not entitled to raise an action of unfair dismissal in the courts. The reason is that Parliament intended for unfair dismissal claims to be dealt with by specialist employment tribunals who are experienced in the resolution of such disputes. Section 111(2) of the ERA 1996 directs that the employee must present the complaint to an employment tribunal within three months of the effective date of termination of his or her contract of employment or within such further period as the tribunal considers reasonable in a case where it is satisfied that it was not reasonably practicable for the complaint to be presented within the three-month time limit.

Automatically unfair dismissals

Where any of the following criteria are met (this list is not exhaustive), a dismissal will be automatically unfair and the qualifying period of two years' continuous employment of the employee in section 108(1) of the ERA 1996 is irrelevant in such circumstances:

- The employee is dismissed on the basis that he or she was a member of a trade union or was not a member of a trade union – section 152 of the Trade Union and Labour Relations (Consolidation) Act 1992.
- The employee is dismissed for a reason connected with pregnancy, childbirth or maternity – section 99 of the ERA 1996.
- The employee is dismissed for a reason connected with health and safety, e.g. where an employee makes a complaint to his or her employer about a breach of health and safety laws – section 100 of the ERA 1996.
- The employee is dismissed for taking action to exercise one of his or her rights under the Working Time Regulations 1998, e.g. a breach of the 48-hour working week – section 101A of the ERA 1996.
- The employee is dismissed for asserting one of his or her statutory rights, e.g. an employee's statutory right to time off work to look after dependants under section 57A of the ERA 1996 – section 104 of the ERA 1996.

■ The meaning of 'dismissal'

There are three types of 'dismissal'. If an employee cannot show that he has been 'dismissed', his claim for unfair dismissal will be ruled out by an employment tribunal.

KEY STATUTE

ERA 1996, s. 95(1)

. . . an employee is dismissed by his employer if –

(a) the contract under which he is employed is terminated by the employer (whether with or without notice),

(b) he is employed under a limited-term contract and that contract terminates by virtue of the limiting event without being renewed under the same contract, or

(c) the employee terminates the contract under which he is employed (with or without notice) in circumstances in which he is entitled to terminate it without notice by reason of the employer's conduct.

□ REVISION NOTE

Section 95(1)(a) of the ERA 1996 covers a positive act of dismissal by the employer, i.e. where the employer 'fires' the employee. Section 95(1)(b) applies where a **fixed-term contract** comes to its natural end. Finally, section 95(1)(c) describes the constructive dismissal of an employee.

KEY DEFINITION: Fixed-term contract

A contract which endures for a specific period of time and terminates at the end of that period of time.

■ Constructive dismissal

The definition of 'constructive dismissal' is set out in section 95 of the ERA 1996.

KEY STATUTE

ERA 1996, s. 95

(1) For the purposes of this Part an employee is dismissed by his employer if. . .

(c) the employee terminates the contract under which he is employed (with or without notice) in circumstances in which he is entitled to terminate it without notice by reason of the employer's conduct.

The nature of the employer's conduct

Section 95(1)(c) of the ERA 1996 enables an employee to terminate the contract of employment without notice in response to the employer's conduct. The question is what standard of conduct of the employer is relevant for the purposes of the section. The case of *Western Excavating (ECC) Ltd* v *Sharp* (1978) held that whether the employer's conduct was reasonable or unreasonable was not the appropriate test. Instead, the question was whether the employer's conduct:

- amounted to a significant or repudiatory breach of contract going to the root of the contract of employment; or
- demonstrated that the employer no longer intended to be bound by one or more of the essential terms of the contract.

Examples of repudiatory conduct

Some examples of repudiatory conduct are as follows:

- reducing an employee's benefits to a material extent (*Gillies* v *Richard Daniels & Co.* (1979));
- reducing an employee's status or salary (*Coleman* v *S & W Baldwin* (1977) and *Industrial Rubber Products* v *Gillon* (1977));
- any serious breach of the implied terms of the contract of employment, e.g. the implied term of mutual trust and confidence and the implied term to exercise reasonable care.

In such circumstances, the employee is entitled to treat himself or herself as:

- discharged from any further performance;
- constructively dismissed, and can seek compensation.

KEY CASE

Land Securities Trillium Ltd v *Thornley* [2005] IRLR 765

Concerning: repudiatory conduct, constructive dismissal

Facts

Ms Thornley was employed as an in-house architect. Although she had certain management responsibilities, her main duties were those of a 'hands-on' architect. As part of a restructuring, Ms Thornley's duties were altered to a mainly managerial role on the basis of a 'flexibility' clause in her contract of employment. She contended that the alterations were such that she was being asked to perform a different job without her consent. She left her employment and claimed constructive dismissal. ▶

> **Legal principle**
>
> The employer was in fundamental breach of her contract of employment in imposing a new job description. The job description changed her duties from a hands-on role to a mainly managerial one and had the effect of deskilling her as an architect. Accordingly, she had been constructively dismissed.

Stages involved in constructive dismissal

See Figure 9.1 for a description of the relevant issues which are taken into account where an employee makes a complaint of constructive dismissal. From Figure 9.1, you will note that it is crucial that the employee accepts the employer's repudiatory breach of contract at stage 3. It has been held that it is not open to an employer to 'cure' or 'rectify' its repudiatory breach of contract immediately before the occurrence of stage 3: *Buckland* v *Bournemouth University Higher Education Corporation* (2010). For the purposes of stage 3, it is not an absolute requirement that the employee informs the employer at the point he or she leaves employment that the reason that he or she is leaving is the employer's repudiatory breach of contract (*Weathersfield Ltd (t/a Van & Truck Rentals)* v *Sargent* (1999)). With regard to stage 2, where an employee alleges that the employer's conduct was such that it amounted to a breach of the implied term of mutual trust and confidence, the case of *Morrow* v *Safeway Stores plc* (2002) held that this will automatically amount to a repudiatory breach of contract.

> **□ REVISION NOTE**
>
> Whether the employer's conduct is such that the employee is entitled to claim constructive dismissal depends on whether there has been a repudiatory breach of contract on the part of the employer. This, in turn, directs an enquiry as to whether (i) the conduct of the employer is consistent with a repudiatory breach on its part or (ii) an express or implied term of the contract of employment has been seriously breached. As a result, the implied terms which impose duties on the employer which were considered in Chapter 2 assume importance here.

> **□ REVISION NOTE**
>
> It is important that you appreciate that a constructive dismissal is also by definition a wrongful dismissal, i.e. a dismissal in repudiatory breach of the contract of employment. So if an employee can show that the conduct of an employer amounts to a repudiatory breach of contract, he/she must decide whether to raise a wrongful dismissal claim or a constructive dismissal claim. The option he/she chooses will commonly depend on his/her length of service and the level of compensation he/she is seeking. See Figure 8.1 for the differences between a wrongful dismissal claim and an unfair dismissal claim.

Of course, a constructive dismissal is not of itself an unfair dismissal and the employee will need to show that his/her constructive dismissal fell outside the range of reasonable responses open to the employer in terms of section 98(4) of the ERA 1996.

Figure 9.1

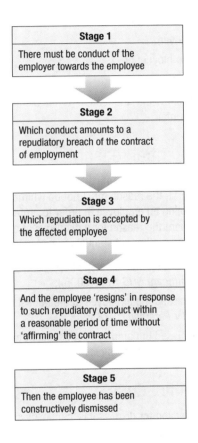

Stage 1

There must be conduct of the employer towards the employee

Stage 2

Which conduct amounts to a repudiatory breach of the contract of employment

Stage 3

Which repudiation is accepted by the affected employee

Stage 4

And the employee 'resigns' in response to such repudiatory conduct within a reasonable period of time without 'affirming' the contract

Stage 5

Then the employee has been constructively dismissed

Affirmation

If an employee approves the contract of employment notwithstanding the employer's conduct (which amounts to a repudiatory breach) then he will be deemed to have waived his right to claim constructive dismissal. Such approval is called 'affirmation' of the contract of employment. Whether the employee has affirmed is a matter of fact and degree. For example, in the case of *Simms* v *Sainsbury's Supermarkets Ltd* (2005), the EAT held that a delay of 10 weeks between the date of the employer's repudiatory breach and the date the employee left employment was too long. Hence, there had been affirmation by the employee. As a result, there had been no constructive dismissal.

▪ The five potentially fair reasons for dismissal

Section 98(1), (2) and (3) provide five potentially fair reasons for dismissal. An employer must show that the reason it dismissed an employee was for one of the following five reasons:

- 'some other substantial reason';
- the 'capability or qualifications' of the employee;
- the 'conduct' of the employee;
- the **redundancy** of the employee; or
- the contravention of a duty or statute.

If the employer is unable to show that the reason for the dismissal is one of the above, the dismissal will be held to be unfair.

'Some other substantial reason'

What factual circumstances amount to 'some other substantial reason' in terms of section 98(1)(b) of the ERA 1996? First, the reason must not be whimsical. Secondly, most cases involve the employer dismissing an employee in order to protect its legitimate business interests. Circumstances where the reason for a dismissal of an employee have been held by the tribunals to constitute 'some other substantial reason' have been as follows:

- where an employee was found to have a difficult personality or unfortunate manner (*Perkin* v *St George's Healthcare NHS Trust* (2005));
- where the employer dismissed the employee at the behest of its key client (*Scott Packing and Warehousing Co. Ltd* v *Paterson* (1978));
- where the employer dismissed the employee subsequent to a corporate takeover (*Cobley* v *Forward Technology Industries plc* (2003)).

'Capability or qualifications'

The second potentially fair reason for dismissal is 'capability or qualifications'. This involves the illness, poor performance, incompetence or lack of qualifications of an employee. See Figure 9.2 for clarification of the relevant issues to take into account in respect of incompetence and ill health.

'Conduct'/misconduct

The third potentially fair reason is the 'conduct' of the employee, i.e. gross or serious misconduct (e.g. fighting, intoxication and theft in the workplace), breaches of discipline or procedure or the commission of criminal offences. See Figure 9.3 for clarification of the relevant issues in respect of misconduct.

Redundancy

Redundancy is the fourth potentially fair reason and will be considered in detail in Chapter 10.

Breach or contravention of a duty or statute

The final potentially fair reason is breach or contravention of a duty or statute. A simple example is where the driver of an HGV is disqualified from driving.

Figure 9.2

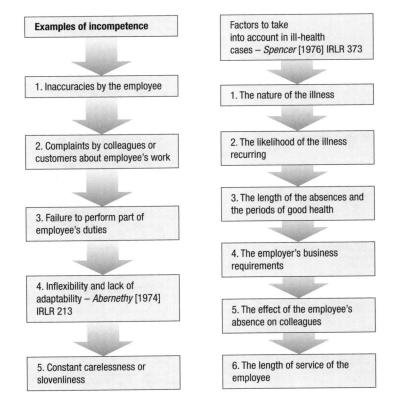

Examples of incompetence
1. Inaccuracies by the employee
2. Complaints by colleagues or customers about employee's work
3. Failure to perform part of employee's duties
4. Inflexibility and lack of adaptability – *Abernethy* [1974] IRLR 213
5. Constant carelessness or slovenliness

Factors to take into account in ill-health cases – *Spencer* [1976] IRLR 373
1. The nature of the illness
2. The likelihood of the illness recurring
3. The length of the absences and the periods of good health
4. The employer's business requirements
5. The effect of the employee's absence on colleagues
6. The length of service of the employee

■ The 'range of reasonable responses' test

Once the employer has shown that the reason for the dismissal of the employee was one of the above five reasons, it must satisfy the employment tribunal that its decision to dismiss fell within the band of reasonable responses open to it.

ERA 1996, s. 98

(4) In any other case where the employer has fulfilled the requirements of subsection (1) the determination of the question whether the dismissal is fair or unfair (having regard to the reason shown by the employer) –

   (a) depends on whether in the circumstances (including the size and administrative resources of the employer's undertaking) the employer acted reasonably or unreasonably in treating it as a sufficient reason for dismissing the employee, and

   (b) shall be determined in accordance with equity and the substantial merits of the case.

Figure 9.3

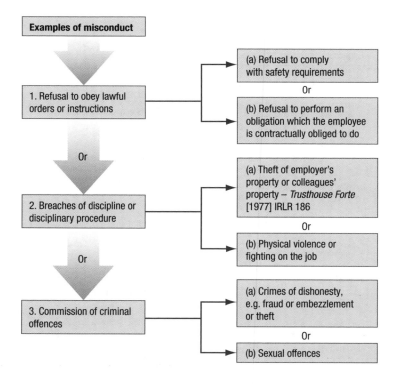

The reasonableness or unreasonableness of the employer

In construing whether a dismissal is fair or unfair, the tribunals apply the 'range of reasonable responses' test. Instead of the tribunal or court enquiring whether the employer's decision to dismiss was reasonable or unreasonable on a purely objective basis and thus substituting its own judgment for that of the employer, the tribunal must ask whether dismissal was one of the reasonable responses which reasonable employers might take to the act complained of, the events which occurred or the reason for the employee's dismissal. For an example of the range of reasonable responses test in operation, see Figure 9.4.

Figure 9.4

Case study No. 1
Scenario: Employee is dismissed for misconduct for claiming travel expenses of £600 when she submits only £580 of receipts. Employer's investigation reveals no suggestion of fraud.
Question: What are the reasonable responses of an employer to this event/reason?
Employment tribunal identifies three reasonable responses: 1. Employer takes no action. 2. Employer issues a verbal warning. 3. Employer obtains employee's agreement to the deduction of £20 from her wages.
Outcome: Since dismissal is not identified as a reasonable response, dismissal is prima facie unfair.

Case study No. 2
Scenario: Employee is dismissed on capability grounds. Employee is a doctor and performed surgery on a patient's wrong kidney.
Question: What are the reasonable responses of an employer to this event/reason?
Employment tribunal identifies two reasonable responses: 1. Dismissal 2. Final written warning
Outcome: Since dismissal is identified as a reasonable response, dismissal is prima facie fair.

British Home Stores Ltd v *Burchell* [1978] IRLR 379

Concerning: 'range of reasonable responses' test, misconduct of employee

Facts

Burchell was dismissed for allegedly being involved with a number of other employees in acts of dishonesty relating to staff purchases. The employer conducted an investigation into allegations of irregularities and during the investigation Burchell was implicated by another of the employees involved.

Legal principle

The EAT held that Burchell's dismissal was not unfair. The 'range of reasonable responses' test was applied by the EAT. Guidance on the approach which tribunals should take in cases of misconduct was elaborated upon as follows:

(1) the employer must demonstrate that it believed that the employee was guilty of the relevant misconduct at the time it took the decision to dismiss;

(2) the employer must demonstrate that it had in mind reasonable grounds upon which to sustain that belief; and

(3) the employer, at the stage at which it formed that belief on those grounds, and at any rate at the final stage at which it formed that belief on those grounds, must have carried out as much investigation into the matter as was reasonable in all the circumstances of the case.

✎ EXAM TIP

A problem question may ask you to consider a set of facts and circumstances relating to an individual employee who has been dismissed. In answering the problem question and analysing whether the dismissal is fair or unfair, you should concentrate on the reason for the dismissal and ask what the responses of a reasonable employer to that reason or act would have been. As shown in Figure 9.4, you should then jot down what those reasonable responses might be. If dismissal does not feature within the range, i.e. it is not on your list then the dismissal is unfair.

 Make your answer stand out

Judicial and academic commentators have criticised the 'range of reasonable responses' test and the hurdles which it places in front of dismissed employees. In order to gain extra marks in an exam answer, you should consider whether you agree with Collins (2000: 294) that 'in practice, it often degenerates into a test of perversity . . . [and] upholds the justice of dismissals that are "harsh but fair"'. See also Collins (2004).

◼ Fair and proper dismissal and disciplinary procedures and policies

Where an employer fails to comply with fair and proper disciplinary procedures in advance of dismissing an employee, an employment tribunal is very likely to hold that the dismissal was procedurally irregular and that it amounted to an unfair dismissal. The disciplinary procedures applied by the employer may be contractual in the sense that they are conferred contractual status in terms of the employee's contract of employment. Alternatively, the disciplinary procedures may be non-contractual. The content of those contractual or non-contractual disciplinary procedures are often based on the ACAS Code of Practice 1 on Disciplinary and Grievance Procedures (see http://www.acas.org.uk/media/pdf/f/m/Acas-Code-of-Practice-1-on-disciplinary-and-grievance-procedures.pdf for a copy). Section 207A(1) and (2) of, and Schedule A2 to, the Trade Union and Labour Relations (Consolidation) Act 1992 provides that an employer's unreasonable failure to comply with the provisions of the ACAS Code of Practice 1 on Disciplinary and Grievance Procedures may be taken into

Figure 9.5

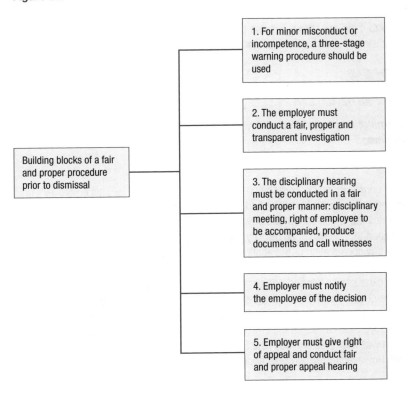

Building blocks of a fair and proper procedure prior to dismissal

1. For minor misconduct or incompetence, a three-stage warning procedure should be used

2. The employer must conduct a fair, proper and transparent investigation

3. The disciplinary hearing must be conducted in a fair and proper manner: disciplinary meeting, right of employee to be accompanied, produce documents and call witnesses

4. Employer must notify the employee of the decision

5. Employer must give right of appeal and conduct fair and proper appeal hearing

account by an ET, as a means of increasing any compensation award against the employer by no more than 25 per cent.

Tribunals are extremely clear that the application of good industrial practice – and the compliance of employers with fair and reasonable dismissal procedures – is crucial to a finding of fair dismissal. The upshot of this is that if the employer's decision to dismiss is found to fall within the band of reasonable responses, the dismissal will nevertheless be deemed to be unfair if the employer failed to follow fair and proper non-statutory dismissal procedures. See Figure 9.5 for the basic building blocks of such a fair and proper procedure.

The effect of *Polkey*

In *Polkey* v *AE Dayton Services Ltd* (1987), the House of Lords held that a dismissal would be unfair, even where an employer could show that:

- the (i) decision to dismiss and (ii) investigation, which it undertook in respect of the behaviour of the employee prior to the dismissal, fell within the range of reasonable responses;
- although it did not follow fair and proper procedures, it would have made no difference to its decision to dismiss if it had done so.

KEY CASE

Polkey v *AE Dayton Services Ltd* **[1987] IRLR 503**

Concerning: employer's 'no difference' argument, importance of pre-dismissal procedures

Facts

Without prior warning or consultation, an employee was called into his employer's branch manager's office and told that he had been made redundant. A redundancy letter was handed to him, which set out the payments due to him and he was sent home. The employee complained that he had been unfairly dismissed because he had been made redundant without any consultation or the application of any pre-dismissal procedure. The employer argued that it would have made no difference to its decision to make the employee redundant if it had exhausted a fair and proper pre-dismissal procedure prior to the employee's dismissal. The industrial tribunal agreed with the employer and ruled that the employee had not been unfairly dismissed since it concluded that the result would have been the same if the employer had consulted the employee and applied a proper pre-dismissal procedure. The decision was appealed and both the EAT and the Court of Appeal dismissed the employee's appeal. However, the employee's appeal to the House of Lords was allowed. ▶

Legal principle

The House of Lords rejected the 'no difference' argument, thus strengthening the importance attached to pre-dismissal procedures. It held that it is no defence to a finding that (i) the dismissal was unfair and (ii) the dismissal and antecedent disciplinary procedures applied were improper and irregular, for an employer to argue that the application of proper and regular procedures would have made no difference to its decision to dismiss. However, as we will see in Chapter 10, the 'no difference' argument will be taken into account for the purposes of reducing the compensatory award paid to the unfairly dismissed employee.

■ Putting it all together

Answer guidelines

See the essay question at the start of this chapter. A diagram illustrating how to structure your answer is available on the website.

Approaching the question

This question requires you to address and analyse the range of reasonable responses test. It is crucial that you first explore the definition of a dismissal and the five potentially valid reasons for dismissal. See below for further details.

Important points to include

Points to remember when answering this question:

- In your introduction, you should explore the preliminary stages of an unfair dismissal claim, i.e. (i) whether there has been a 'dismissal' in terms of section 95(1) of the ERA 1996 and (ii) whether the employer's reason for the dismissal was one of the five potentially fair reasons.
- You should spell out the method of enforcement of unfair dismissal claims, i.e. through the employment tribunal system.
- You should display an understanding of the automatically unfair dismissals.
- Consider the importance of the application of fair and proper disciplinary procedures.

▶

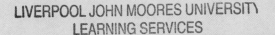

Make your answer stand out

- Address whether you believe that the range of reasonable responses test is a perversity test.

- Examine other tests which could, or perhaps ought to, replace the range of reasonable responses test – e.g. a proportionality test – and what this would mean.

READ TO IMPRESS

Anderman, S. (2004) Termination of employment: whose property rights? in C. Barnard, S. Deakin and G. Morris (eds), *The Future of Labour Law: Liber Amicorum Bob Hepple QC*, Oxford: Hart, 103.

Collins, H. (1992) *Justice in Dismissal*, Oxford: Clarendon Press.

Collins, H. (2000) Finding the right direction for the industrial jury. 29 *Industrial Law Journal*: 288.

Collins, H. (2004) *Nine Proposals for the Reform of the Law on Unfair Dismissal*, London: Institute of Employment Rights.

Collins, H. and Freedland, M. (2000) Finding the right direction for the 'industrial jury': *Haddon* v *Van den Bergh Foods Ltd/Midland Bank plc* v *Madden*. 29 *Industrial Law Journal*: 288.

Elias, P. (1981) Fairness in unfair dismissal: trends and tensions. 10 *Industrial Law Journal*: 201.

Freer, A. (1998) The range of reasonable responses test: from guidelines to statute. 27 *Industrial Law Journal*: 336.

www.pearsoned.co.uk/lawexpress

Go online to access more revision support including quizzes to test your knowledge, sample questions with answer guidelines, podcasts you can download, and more!

10

Unfair dismissal (2): remedies and redundancy

■ Topic map

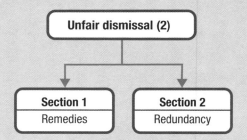

■ Introduction

An employee has a statutory right not to be unfairly dismissed on the basis of redundancy.

This chapter examines the remedies available to an employee where an employment tribunal makes a finding that the employee has been unfairly dismissed. It analyses the main remedy, which is the remedy of compensation and as such, this chapter should be read closely in conjunction with Chapter 9. Finally, the important topic of redundancy will be considered.

ASSESSMENT ADVICE

Essay questions

Essay questions require broad general knowledge of the remedies for unfair dismissal that are made available to employees. You will also be expected to understand the statutory definition of 'redundancy', since it constitutes one of the five statutory potentially fair reasons for dismissal. An appreciation of the issues the tribunals will take into account in determining whether an individual has been made redundant and whether the redundancy was fair is also essential.

Problem questions

These may involve an examination of a particular individual employee's or employer's factual circumstances with a view to determining whether that individual has a reasonable prospect of success in pursuing an unfair dismissal claim on the basis that he or she has not been made redundant. In answering a problem question, you should also be able to assess whether the facts amount to an unfair redundancy and whether the individual who has been dismissed satisfies the definition of 'redundancy' in section 139 of the ERA 1996.

■ Sample question

Could you answer this question? Below is a typical problem question that could arise on this topic. Guidelines on answering the question are included at the end of the chapter, while a sample essay question and guidance on tackling it can be found on the companion website.

PROBLEM QUESTION

Glenn Bristow has been employed by FictitiousCorp Ltd as a human resources assistant for six years. He is appraised by his employer every three months and his past nine appraisals have pointed to less than satisfactory performance. Glenn has been issued with appropriate performance criteria after each appraisal. Issues such as his timekeeping, attention to detail and interpersonal skills have consistently been graded poorly and remain a concern. FictitiousCorp Ltd announces that it is to make 15 people redundant (out of a workforce of 500 employees) in its human resources department owing to a slowdown in sales, and Glenn is earmarked for redundancy. The selection criterion applied by FictitiousCorp Ltd is past performance. Hence, this is the reason why Glenn is selected as one of the unlucky 15. Glenn is not offered suitable alternative employment by FictitiousCorp Ltd. He is not consulted about the proposed redundancy. When he is made redundant and receives a redundancy payment based on the statutory criteria, he seeks your advice regarding his position. Advise Glenn.

◼ Remedies for unfair dismissal

There are three remedies available where an employee has been held to have been unfairly dismissed namely reinstatement, re-engagement (see section 113 of the ERA 1996) or compensation. Reinstatement involves the reversal of the dismissal so that the employee gets his or her old job back. Re-engagement is slightly different and describes the situation where an employee is re-employed by his or her employer but works in a different job.

Compensation

In approximately 95 per cent of cases in which employees are successful in their unfair dismissal claim, compensation will be the remedy awarded by the employment tribunal. Compensation involves the employee being awarded a basic award and a compensatory award. The basic award is a fixed figure which can be calculated according to the employee's length of continuous service and age. At the time of writing, the maximum amount payable is £14,370, but such maximum limit is increased annually. The maximum compensatory award is currently fixed at £78,962, or 12 months' salary, whichever is the lower. Like the basic award, this maximum figure is increased every year. The amount of the compensatory award is defined by section 123 of the ERA 1996. Section 124A of the

ERA 1996 provides that the compensatory award may be increased by up to 25 per cent where the employer has failed to comply with ACAS's Code of Practice on Disciplinary and Grievance Procedures in advance of a dismissal (see http://www.acas.org.uk/media/pdf/f/m/Acas-Code-of-Practice-1-on-disciplinary-and-grievance-procedures.pdf for a copy).

KEY STATUTE

ERA 1996, s. 123

(1) . . . the amount of the compensatory award shall be such amount as the tribunal considers just and equitable in all the circumstances having regard to the loss sustained by the complainant in consequence of the dismissal in so far as that loss is attributable to action taken by the employer.

(2) The loss referred to in subsection (1) shall be taken to include –

   (a) any expenses reasonably incurred by the complainant in consequence of the dismissal, and

   (b) subject to subsection (3), loss of any benefit which he might reasonably be expected to have had but for the dismissal. . .

The tribunals and courts have consistently pronounced that the purpose of the compensatory award is to compensate the employee for his or her financial loss. Its objective is not to penalise the employer for any fault on its part in dismissing the employee.

! Don't be tempted to . . .

Don't be fooled into thinking that the word 'loss' in section 123 of the ERA 1996 is given a wide interpretation by the tribunals and courts. In *Dunnachie* v *Kingston-Upon-Hull City Council* (2004), the House of Lords held that it was not competent to award compensation for losses suffered by the employee in respect of injury to feelings. The word 'loss' in section 123 of the ERA 1996 was restricted to economic losses of the employee. Do you agree with this? In the breach of contract case of *Farley* v *Skinner* (2001), the House of Lords held that damages for non-monetary losses may be awarded to the innocent party in a breach of contract. You should consider *Farley* and whether the ratio in that case can be used as a basis to critique the reasoning of the House of Lords in *Dunnachie* or not.

■ Redundancy

As mentioned in Chapter 9, **redundancy** is one of the five potentially fair reasons for dismissal. It occurs when an employer needs to dismiss employees for economic reasons, e.g. a downturn in business.

Right to receive a redundancy payment

A redundant employee who has been continuously employed for a period of two years or more has the right to receive a redundancy payment.

KEY STATUTE

ERA 1996, s. 135

(1) An employer shall pay a redundancy payment to any employee of his if the employee –

    (a) is dismissed by the employer by reason of redundancy. . .

ERA 1996, s. 155

An employee does not have any right to a redundancy payment unless he has been continuously employed for a period of not less than two years ending with the relevant date.

Calculation of statutory redundancy payment

The statutory redundancy payment is calculated as follows:

- a half week's pay for each full year of service where the employee's age during the year is less than 22 years of age;
- one week's pay for each full year of service where the employee's age during the year is 22 years or above, but less than 41 years;
- one-and-a-half weeks' pay for each full year of service where the employee's age during the year is 41 years or above.

In other words, it is calculated in exactly the same manner as the basic award in the context of unfair dismissal. At the time of writing, the maximum amount payable is £14,370, but such maximum limit is increased annually. See above for further details.

📖 REVISION NOTE

In problem questions, you should ensure that it is stated that the employee has been continuously employed for at least two years. Otherwise, the employee will not be entitled to a redundancy payment. Furthermore, if an employee rejects suitable alternative employment, which is offered by the employer, that employee will forfeit his or her right to a redundancy payment (sections 138 and 141 of the ERA 1996).

Definition of 'redundancy'

Redundancy is defined in section 139(1) of the ERA 1996.

KEY STATUTE

ERA 1996, s. 139(1)

. . . an employee who is dismissed shall be taken to be dismissed by reason of redundancy if the dismissal is wholly or mainly attributable to –

(a) the fact that his employer has ceased or intends to cease –

    (i)   to carry on the business for the purposes of which the employee was employed by him, or

    (ii) to carry on that business in the place where the employee was so employed, or

(b) the fact that the requirements of that business –

    (i)   for employees to carry out work of a particular kind, or

    (ii) for employees to carry out work of a particular kind in the place where the employee was employed by the employer,

have ceased or diminished or are expected to cease or diminish.

Diminishing requirements – 'work of a particular kind'

Section 139(1)(a)(i) of the ERA 1996 applies where there is a permanent or temporary cessation of the employer's business, i.e. the employer stops trading. Section 139(1)(a)(ii) of the ERA 1996 applies where the employer ceases to carry on its business in a particular place, e.g. the closure of a branch, office or factory. The test of diminishing requirements in section 139(1)(b) of the ERA 1996 has been the most troublesome of the tests in section 139(1) of the ERA 1996 for the courts and tribunals to apply. Essentially, it seeks to cover the situation where the employer has surplus labour, i.e. it requires fewer employees for existing work or there is less work for existing employees. Two schools of thought emerged as to how courts and tribunals should ascertain whether the employer's requirements for 'work of a particular kind' had ceased or diminished. The first was the 'contract' test, which considered the work which the employee was under a duty to do under the terms of his or her contract of employment. The second was the 'function' test which instead looked at the work which the employee actually did. Different cases applied different tests, but the matter was settled by the House of Lords in *Murray* v *Foyle Meats Ltd* (1999).

KEY CASE

Murray v *Foyle Meats Ltd* [1999] IRLR 56

Concerning: 'work of a particular kind', redundancy

Facts

Murray was employed as a meat plant operative in a slaughter hall which was located in the employer's factory. Owing to a downturn in business, the employer decided that there was a need to reduce the number of skilled meat plant operatives working in the slaughter hall. After a selection process, Murray was dismissed for redundancy and he claimed that the definition of redundancy in section 139(1)(b) of the ERA 1996 had not been satisfied.

Legal principle

The House of Lords rejected Murray's appeal. The definition of redundancy in section 139(1)(b) of the ERA 1996 was simple and asked two questions of fact. The first is whether one or other of various states of economic affairs exists. In this case, this was whether the requirements of the business for employees to carry out work of a particular kind had diminished. The second question is whether the applicant's dismissal was attributable, wholly or mainly, to that state of affairs. Hence, the matter is one of factual causation and is for the tribunal to determine. The House of Lords criticised both the 'contract' and 'function' tests.

 Make your answer stand out

Students who address whether they agree with the decision of the House of Lords in *Murray* would be going above and beyond what is asked and would be likely to gain some extra marks. For example, do you agree that the 'contract' and 'function' tests miss the point of section 139(1)(b) of the ERA 1996? If so, what is the purpose of the words 'work of a particular kind' in that subsection? See Anderman (2000) and Deakin and Morris (2012).

'Pools' and selection criteria and procedures

In deciding which of the members of the workforce are to be made redundant, the employer must:

■ choose an appropriate pool of employees for redundancy;
■ apply fair and proper selection criteria and procedures to the chosen pool.

An appropriate pool is one where the range of jobs in the pool is interchangeable. A fair and proper selection procedure is where employees are graded according to skills, performance, timekeeping, work attendance, abilities and other neutral objective criteria, and the application of such objective criteria can be verified against written documentation (e.g. see *British Aerospace plc* v *Green* (1995) and *E-ZEC Medical Transport Service Ltd* v *Gregory* (2008)). If the employer has chosen to make 10 employees redundant from a pool of clerical staff, then employees in clerical positions with the lowest 10 scores would be made redundant. The employer must be able to verify that those employees were selected objectively. Provided the process is open and transparent, the benefit of such an approach is that it is based on meritocratic, rather than discriminatory, criteria (see Chapters 5 and 6).

Offer of suitable alternative employment

Part of the process of fair and proper selection of employees for redundancy is for the employer to consider suitable alternative employment which might be offered to selected employees. For example, if it is proposed to make a PA redundant, the employer should consider whether a secretarial post might be made available and offered to the PA. A failure on the part of the employer to consider such possible suitable alternatives may result in a finding of unfair dismissal.

Consultation procedures

It is incumbent on an employer to consult with the affected employees and employee representatives or trade unions and to comply with good industrial relations practice. A failure to consult with individual employees earmarked for possible redundancy about the selection process and criteria prior to the decision to dismiss that employee for the reason of redundancy is likely to result in a finding of unfair dismissal (see *E-ZEC Medical Transport Service Ltd* v *Gregory* (2008)).

Good industrial practice

1. As much warning as possible of the proposed redundancies should be given to employees and trade unions to enable meaningful, fair and genuine consultation to take place.

2. The consultation process itself must be fair, meaningful and genuine.

3. Consultation must take place with the individual employees affected, as well as employee representatives and trade unions.

4. If there are no selection criteria in a redundancy agreement or collective agreement, the selection criteria should be agreed with the trade unions or employee representatives.

5. The selection criteria should be transparent, objective, verifiable against documentation, fair and proper and applied properly by the employer.

6. Suitable alternative employment should be considered and, if there is any, duly offered to the selected employees.

📖 REVISION NOTE

In Chapter 9, we referred to the rule in *Polkey* v *AE Dayton Services Ltd* (1987) that an employer will not be able to avoid a finding of unfair dismissal if it can demonstrate that:

- the decision to dismiss fell within the range of reasonable responses;
- its failure to follow a proper procedure in respect of the dismissal would have made no difference to its decision to dismiss.

The same rule applies in the context of redundancy.

✎ EXAM TIP

In problem questions, you may be asked whether an individual has been unfairly dismissed for the reason of redundancy. In coming to a view, you should consider whether the facts in the problem state that:

- meaningful, fair and genuine consultation has taken place between the employer and employee, employee representatives and trade union;
- the employer has offered the employee suitable alternative employment;
- a pool has been chosen and that selection procedures have been agreed and properly applied to that pool.

Some of these issues will require you to make a judgement (e.g. the nature of the pool and the selection procedure and whether they are fair, objective and transparent) rather than a purely factual assessment.

■ Putting it all together

Answer guidelines

See the problem question at the start of this chapter. A diagram illustrating how to structure your answer is available on the website.

Approaching the question

The focus in this question is on whether the employer has complied with a fair and proper procedure prior to Glenn's redundancy. See below for further details.

Important points to include

Points to remember when answering this question:

- The first major issue is to consider whether the definition of 'redundancy' contained in section 139(1) of the ERA 1996 has been satisfied in the employee's case.
- You should examine whether the chosen pool for comparison is fair and proper.
- Analyse whether 'past performance' is a fair, proper, objective and neutral selection criterion.
- Explain the effect of the employer's failure to consult with the employee (generally, or about the selection procedure to be applied) or to offer the employee suitable alternative employment.
- If the employer argues that it would have made no difference to its decision to select the employee for redundancy if it had consulted with him or her about the proposed redundancy in advance, would such an argument result in a finding that the redundancy was fair?

 Make your answer stand out

Consider the implications of *Murray* v *Foyle Meats Ltd* (1999).

READ TO IMPRESS

Anderman, S. (2000) The interpretation of protective employment statutes and contracts of employment. 29 *Industrial Law Journal*: 223, 229–233.

Bowers, J. and Lewis, J. (2005) Non-economic damage in unfair dismissal cases: what's left after Dunnachie? 34(1) *Industrial Law Journal*: 83.

Collins, H. (2004) Compensation for the manner of dismissal. 33(2) *Industrial Law Journal*: 152.

Collins, H. (2012) Compensation for dismissal: in search of principle. 41(2) *Industrial Law Journal*: 208.

Deakin, S. and Morris, G. (2012) *Labour Law*, 6th edn, Oxford: Hart, 564–568.

www.pearsoned.co.uk/lawexpress

Go online to access more revision support including quizzes to test your knowledge, sample questions with answer guidelines, podcasts you can download, and more!

11

Collective labour law

Revision checklist

Essential points you should know:

- [ ] The law relating to trade unions
- [ ] The legal protection of trade union membership and activities
- [ ] Collective bargaining and the statutory recognition of trade unions
- [ ] The law of industrial conflict

■ Topic map

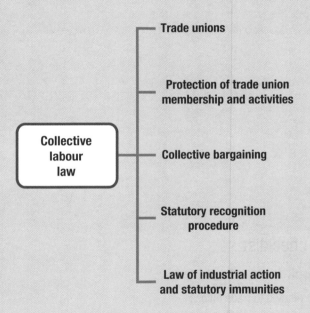

Trade unions

Protection of trade union membership and activities

Collective labour law

Collective bargaining

Statutory recognition procedure

Law of industrial action and statutory immunities

A printable version of this topic map is available from **www.pearsoned.co.uk/lawexpress**

■ Introduction

Trade union members and trade unions enjoy certain protected rights in relation to industrial disputes.

This chapter examines a number of issues which are relevant to collective labour law. The majority of collective labour law is contained in the Trade Union and Labour Relations (Consolidation) Act 1992. First, the institution of the trade union is considered, together with the legal definition of a 'trade union' and the meaning of 'independence' of trade unions. Secondly, the legal protection of trade union membership and activities will be examined. Collective bargaining and the statutory procedures in respect of the recognition of trade unions will be briefly analysed. Finally, the important topic of industrial conflict will be explored.

ASSESSMENT ADVICE

Essay questions

These require broad general knowledge of the rights and duties of trade unions. You must also understand the statutory recognition procedures which apply to trade unions. An appreciation of some of the issues regarding the liability and statutory immunities of trade unions in tort or delict (in Scotland) may also be required. In tackling essay questions, you should always directly answer the question(s) asked and apply the relevant law.

Problem questions

Problem questions may involve an examination of a particular trade union's factual circumstances or an individual employee's or employer's factual circumstances. You will be expected to determine whether the trade union, individual or employer has a reasonable prospect of success in pursuing a claim. In tackling problem questions, you should always directly answer the question(s) asked and apply the relevant law to the facts at hand. For example, if the problem question involves an employee who has been persuaded by a trade union to breach his or her contract of employment with his or her employer, you should seek to ascertain whether the trade union will have committed the tort of inducing a breach of contract and whether the union enjoys statutory immunity from liability.

■ Sample question

Could you answer this question? Below is a typical essay question that could arise on this topic. Guidelines on answering the question are included at the end of the chapter, while a sample problem question and guidance on tackling it can be found on the companion website.

ESSAY QUESTION

Critically evaluate the statutory immunities from liability conferred on trade unions in the Trade Union and Labour Relations (Consolidation) Act 1992. Is the law satisfactory?

■ Trade unions

Definition of a 'trade union' and legal status

If a body falls within the statutory definition of a '**trade union**', certain legal rights and duties will be conferred and imposed upon that body.

KEY STATUTE

Trade Union and Labour Relations (Consolidation) Act 1992 (TULRCA 1992), s. 1

. . . a 'trade union' means an organisation (whether temporary or permanent) –

(a) which consists wholly or mainly of workers of one or more descriptions and whose principal purposes include the regulation of relations between workers of that description or those descriptions and employers or employers' associations . . .

Legal status of trade unions

Under the common law, a trade union was not treated as a body corporate, i.e. a legal body distinct from its member workers. Instead, it was treated as an unincorporated association. As a result, the trade union had no separate legal personality and so could not be sued in its own name and could not enter into contracts or deeds in its own name. The position is now governed by TULRCA 1992, section 10, which ascribes partial, rather than full, corporate status upon a trade union.

TULRCA 1992, s. 10

(1) A trade union is not a body corporate but –

  (a) it is capable of making contracts [in its own name];

  (b) it is capable of suing and being sued in its own name, whether in proceedings relating to property or founded on contract or tort or any other cause of action; and

  (c) proceedings for an offence alleged to have been committed by it or on its behalf may be brought against it in its own name . . .

Section 12(1) of TULRCA 1992 also provides that all property belonging to a trade union shall be vested in trustees in trust for it.

Listing

Section 2 of TULRCA 1992 provides that the Certification Officer must maintain a list of trade unions. Where an organisation applies for listing, the Certification Officer will list the trade union provided that he or she is satisfied that the organisation falls within the definition of a 'trade union' in section 1 of TULRCA 1992. On the application of an organisation whose name is included in the list, the Certification Officer is under an obligation to issue a certificate that the organisation is listed. The Certification Officer is given power by section 4 of TULRCA 1992 to remove an organisation from the list if it appears to him or her that it no longer falls within the definition of a 'trade union'.

Independence

Once an organisation is entered in the list of trade unions, it may apply to the Certification Officer for a certificate of independence. This certificate confirms that the organisation concerned is an 'independent trade union'.

Why is 'independent' status important to a trade union?

There are a number of reasons why a trade union will seek a certificate of independence. Some of the reasons are as follows:

■ employees are treated as automatically unfairly dismissed if they are dismissed for the reason that they are, or propose to become, members of an **independent trade union** (TULRCA 1992, s. 152);

■ 'workers' who are members of an independent trade union will enjoy protection from being subjected to a detriment by their employer on the grounds of their union activities (TULRCA 1992, s. 146);

- independent trade unions enjoy certain tax reliefs and benefits (Income and Corporation Taxes Act 1988, s. 467);
- only independent trade unions may apply for statutory recognition (Para. 6 of Sched. A1 to TULCRA 1992).

KEY DEFINITION: Independent trade union

Section 5 of TULRCA 1992 provides that a trade union is independent if:

(a) it is not under the domination or control of an employer, group of employers or employers' associations; and

(b) it is not liable to interference by an employer (arising out of the provision of financial or material support or by any other means whatsoever) tending towards such control.

 Make your answer stand out

The power and influence of the trade union movement in UK employment relations has decreased significantly over the past 40 years. This is evident from the figures of trade union membership, which declined from 13.2 million members in 1979 to just over 7 million members in 2014/15. Two reasons for this decline are as follows:

- Major structural changes in the UK economy and the composition of the labour market of the UK during the period from 1980 to the present. The UK changed from a manufacturing-based economy to a service-based economy. There was a gradual decline in large manufacturing plants with a large proportion of workers forming part of a union and having one employer. The services sector is more fragmented and the scope for union membership declined.

- The anti-union stance of the Conservative Governments between 1979 and 1997 and the current Government. The Conservative Governments introduced incremental reforms which reduced the power of the trade unions over that period. Examples of such reforms were the restriction of the right of union members to take industrial action, the introduction of ballots for 'closed shops', the disbanding of union recognition machinery and the introduction of rights in favour of union members against trade unions.

In order to gain extra marks in an exam question which asks you to address the role of trade unions in modern Britain, you should consider whether you believe that there is a continuing role for trade unions in the UK in light of the articles by Charlwood (2004) and Ewing (2005).

▉ Protection of trade union membership and activities

Union membership: protection from dismissal and detriment

An employee or worker has the right not to be dismissed or subjected to a detriment on grounds related to trade union membership.

KEY STATUTE

TULRCA 1992, s. 152

(1) . . . the dismissal of an employee shall be regarded as unfair if the reason for it . . . was that the employee –

   (a) was, or proposed to become, a member of an independent trade union. . . or

   (b) was not a member of any trade union, or of a particular trade union . . .

The employee's right under section 152 is enforceable by presenting a complaint to an employment tribunal. If the complaint is successful, the amount of the basic award must not be less than £5,853 (TULRCA 1992, s. 156(1)).

KEY STATUTE

TULRCA 1992, s. 146

(1) A worker has the right not to be subjected to any detriment as an individual by any act, or any deliberate failure to act, by his employer if the act or failure takes place for the sole or main purpose of –

   (a) preventing or deterring him from being or seeking to become a member of an independent trade union, or penalising him for doing so . . . or

   (b) compelling him to be or become a member of any trade union or of a particular trade union . . .

A worker may enforce this right by presenting a complaint to an employment tribunal (TULRCA 1992, s. 146(5)). If the complaint is successful, the employment tribunal will award compensation which it 'considers just and equitable in all the circumstances' having regard to the infringement complained of and to any loss sustained by the worker which is attributable to the act or failure which infringed his or her right (TULRCA 1992, s.149(2)).

! Don't be tempted to . . .

You should not fall into the trap of assuming that threats of the employer to take action are the same as an 'act, or any deliberate failure to act'. The words 'any act, or any deliberate failure to act' in section 146 of TULRCA 1992 cover the conduct and omissions of employers. However, it is not wholly clear whether a threat of adverse consequences by an employer falls within the scope of a detriment. In *Brassington* v *Cauldon Wholesale Ltd* (1977), Bristow J in the EAT did not decide the issue but, from the tenor of his judgment, one can detect a view that a threat of consequences was not the same thing as a detriment or an 'act'. In *Brassington*, the employer had threatened to cease trading, dismiss the whole of the workforce and resume trading under a new name if the workers joined a union. Meanwhile, the jurisprudence of the European Court of Human Rights, e.g. *Young, James and Webster* v *United Kingdom* (1981), suggests that a threat of adverse consequences is an illegitimate interference with the worker's Convention rights to join a trade union and thus is contrary to the ECHR.

📖 REVISION NOTE

The implications of a dismissal being held in law to be an 'automatically unfair dismissal' were covered in Chapter 9.

Union activities: protection from dismissal and detriment

An employee or worker has the right not to be dismissed or subjected to a detriment on grounds related to trade union activities.

KEY STATUTE

TULRCA 1992, s. 152

(1) . . . the dismissal of an employee shall be regarded as unfair if the reason for it . . . was that the employee . . .

    (b) had taken part, or proposed to take part, in the activities of an independent trade union at an appropriate time,

    (ba) had made use, or proposed to make use, of trade union services at an appropriate time . . .

The employee's rights above are also enforceable by presenting a complaint to an employment tribunal. Again, if the complaint is successful, the amount of the basic award must not be less than £5,853 (TULRCA 1992, s. 156(1)).

! **Don't be tempted to . . .**

You ought to avoid making an assumption that participation in industrial action inevitably falls within the compass of the words, 'the activities of an independent trade union'. It is clear from *Drew* v *St Edmundsbury Borough Council* (1980) that participation in industrial action, such as strike action, is not covered by section 152(1)(b) of TULRCA 1992. Moreover, the courts have drawn a distinction between:

1. the situation where a trade union member participates in the kind of activities which his trade union pursues;

2. the situation where a trade union member participates in the kind of activities which (i) his trade union pursues and (ii) the trade union has authorised that member to do on its behalf.

In the case of 1 above, the courts have held that such activity does not fall within section 152(1)(b) of TULRCA 1992, whereas in the case of 2 above, the member will indeed enjoy the protection of section 152(1)(b) – see *Dixon and Shaw* v *West Ella Developments Ltd* (1978).

KEY STATUTE

TULRCA 1992, s. 146

(1) A worker has the right not to be subjected to any detriment as an individual by any act, or any deliberate failure to act, by his employer if the act or failure takes place for the sole or main purpose of

. . .

   (b) preventing or deterring him from taking part in the activities of an independent trade union at an appropriate time, or penalising him for doing so, [or]

   (ba) preventing or deterring him from making use of trade union services at an appropriate time, or penalising him for doing so . . .

Section 146(1)(b) and (ba) of TULRCA 1992 are enforceable in the same fashion as section 152(1)(b) and (ba) of TULRCA 1992 and compensation is also calculated in the same way as section 146(1)(a) and (c).

Inducement not to belong to a trade union

In the case of *Wilson and the NUJ* v *UK* (2002), the European Court of Human Rights held that the UK was in breach of the right to freedom of association under Article 11 of the European Convention on Human Rights by permitting employers to use financial incentives to induce employees to surrender their trade union rights. As a result of this case, the UK Government introduced provisions making such inducements unlawful in sections 145A–145F of TULRCA 1992.

Collective bargaining

One of the primary functions of a trade union is to engage in collective bargaining with an employer or an employers' association. The result of successful collective bargaining is a collective agreement.

Definition of 'collective bargaining'

Collective bargaining is defined in section 178 of TULRCA 1992.

KEY STATUTE

TULRCA 1992, s. 178

(1) . . . 'collective agreement' means any agreement or arrangement made by or on behalf of one or more trade unions and one or more employers or employers' associations and relating to one or more of the matters specified below; and 'collective bargaining' means negotiations relating to or connected with one or more of those matters.

Matters covered by collective bargaining

The matters specified in section 178(2) of TULRCA 1992 are as follows:

- terms and conditions of employment;
- engagement or non-engagement, or termination or suspension of employment or the duties of employment, of one or more workers;
- allocation of work or the duties of employment between workers or groups of workers;
- disciplinary matters;
- a worker's membership or non-membership of a trade union;
- machinery for negotiation or consultation;
- facilities for officials of trade unions.

📖 REVISION NOTE

You should be clear that the definition of 'collective bargaining' in section 178(1) and (2) of TULCRA 1992 is different from the definition of 'collective bargaining' for the purposes of the procedures relating to the statutory recognition of trade unions in Sched. A1 to TULRCA 1992. See Paragraph 3 of Schedule A1 to TULRCA 1992 for the relevant definition in the case of the latter.

There is a presumption that collective agreements are not legally enforceable in a court of law.

KEY STATUTE

TULRCA 1992, s. 179

(1) A collective agreement shall be conclusively presumed not to have been intended by the parties to be a legally enforceable contract unless the agreement –

   (a) is in writing, and

   (b) contains a provision which (however expressed) states that the parties intend that the agreement shall be a legally enforceable contract.

(2) A collective agreement which does satisfy those conditions shall be conclusively presumed to have been intended by the parties to be a legally enforceable contract.

There is a major exception to this rule which we will consider below in the context of the statutory recognition procedure that applies to independent trade unions.

Implications of 'collective bargaining' and collective agreements

Where an independent trade union and employers' association are engaged in collective bargaining, there are certain legal implications, as follows:

- subject to certain limited exceptions, an employer is under a duty to disclose to union representatives (authorised by the union to carry out collective bargaining), on request, certain information, including:
  - information without which the trade union representative would be to a material extent impeded in carrying on collective bargaining with the employer;
  - information which it would be in accordance with good industrial relations practice that the employer should disclose to the trade union representative for the purposes of collective bargaining (sections 181 and 182 of TULRCA 1992);

■ subject to an exception, any term of a collective agreement which prohibits or restricts the right of workers to engage in strike action or other industrial action is treated as not forming part of any contract between the worker and his employer.

▓ Statutory recognition

Application for recognition

Section 70A of and Schedule A1 to TULRCA 1992 outline a procedure for the statutory recognition of trade unions. (See Figure 11.1 for a diagram outlining the principal stages in the recognition procedure.) A trade union may make a request for statutory recognition which entitles it to conduct collective bargaining on behalf of a 'bargaining unit'. A 'bargaining unit' is a group of workers. Initially, a request must be made to the employer for recognition. If the employer refuses the request and the parties are thus unable to agree recognition voluntarily at this stage, the trade union may apply to the Central Arbitration Committee (CAC). The trade union's application will seek a declaration from the CAC awarding it recognition for the purposes of collective bargaining in respect of the specified 'bargaining unit'. The CAC's decision will depend on the degree of support which the union commands within the relevant bargaining unit. The level of support is usually gauged by a secret ballot of all of the workers in the unit. If a majority of the votes cast are in favour of recognition and the number of votes cast represents at least 40 per cent of the total number of workers in the bargaining unit, the CAC will award recognition by declaration. Otherwise, the CAC will issue a declaration that the trade union has no right to recognition.

Collective bargaining

Where a trade union is recognised, it may then conduct 'collective bargaining' with an employer or employers' association. It is important to stress that 'collective bargaining' has a more limited meaning than 'collective bargaining' for the purposes of section 178 of TULRCA 1992. Paragraphs 2 and 3 of Schedule A1 to TULRCA 1992 specifically provide that references to collective bargaining are limited to 'negotiations relating to pay, hours and holidays'. This is subject to Paragraph 4, which empowers the union and the employer to add to these matters by agreement.

Method of collective bargaining

Once a trade union has been recognised, its members may negotiate with the employer about the 'method by which they will conduct collective bargaining [with the employer]' (Para. 30 of Sched. A1) during the 30-day period commencing the day after the CAC issued the declaration of recognition, or some other longer period mutually agreed by the parties. If the parties are unable to agree the method of collective bargaining within this period,

Figure 11.1

Statutory recognition procedure

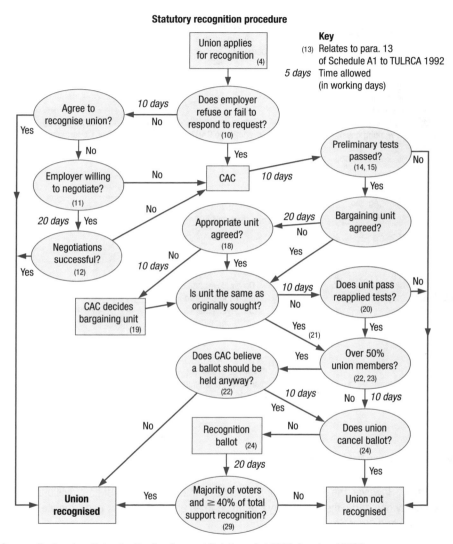

Source: Explanatory Notes for the Employment Relations Act 1999, London: HMSO

any one of the parties may ask the CAC to specify that method which will bind the parties, subject to variation by mutual agreement in writing. See Figure 11.2 for a diagram which outlines the procedure for agreeing the 'method of collective bargaining'.

The 'method of collective bargaining' imposed by the CAC under Schedule A1 to TULRCA 1992 'is to have effect as if it were contained in a legally enforceable contract made by

Figure 11.2

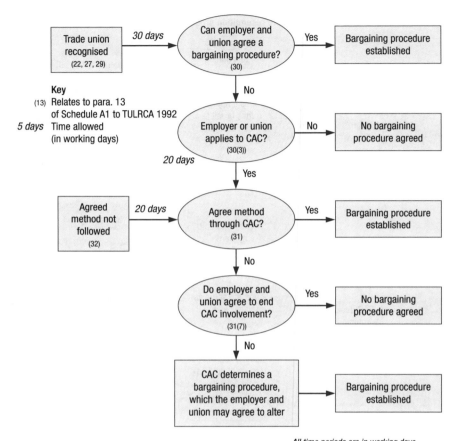

All time periods are in working days

Source: Explanatory Notes for the Employment Relations Act 1999, London: HMSO

the parties'. However, the remedies for breach are limited. Where any of its provisions are breached by one party, the other party is entitled to an order of specific performance only (Para. 31(4) and (6) of Sched. A1).

📖 **REVISION NOTE**

The legal position of such methods of collective bargaining can be contrasted with collective agreements concluded between an employer and trade union generally. You will recall that under section 179 of TULRCA 1992, collective agreements are presumed not to be legally binding.

The issues covered by the 'method of collective bargaining'

Here, we are concerned with the procedure to be applied by the trade union and the employer for the purposes of conducting negotiations during the period of the statutory recognition arrangements. The 'method' imposes a duty to meet each other and discuss issues. It imposes neither a duty on the parties to reach agreement, nor a duty to enter into negotiations with a view to reaching agreement. Issues such as when negotiations are to take place, where they are to take place, which individuals ought to attend are all covered within the 'method'. A model 'method of collective bargaining' is outlined in the Trade Union Recognition (Method of Collective Bargaining) Order 2000, which is a useful reference source.

■ Industrial action and statutory immunities

Examples of industrial action

Examples include the following:

- strike action (a complete, but temporary, withdrawal of labour);
- work to rule (where the workforce observes the letter of the employer's rule book or procedures, rather than the spirit, thus leading to the disruption of the employer's business);
- go-slow action (where the workforce carry out their duties with an appreciable lack of haste, resulting in delays and disruption to the employer's business) and bans on the fulfilment of certain duties.

Industrial action may be lawful or unlawful. Most industrial action in the UK is currently unlawful, i.e. some form of civil liability (e.g. contractual or tortious) will attach to the trade union or the workers engaged in industrial action. This is often the case despite the existence of the statutory immunities.

> **KEY DEFINITION: Industrial action**
>
> Action taken by members of a trade union which imposes restrictions upon employers when collective relations between the employer and the workforce break down.

Liability in tort

Industrial action may lead to civil liability on the part of a trade union. The most common civil liability is tortious liability. This includes:

- the important tort of inducement to commit a breach of contract;
- the tort of causing loss to a third party by unlawful means;

- the tort of intimidation;
- the tort of conspiracy.

This revision guide concentrates on the torts of (i) inducement to commit a breach of contract and (ii) causing loss to a third party by unlawful means.

Inducement to commit a breach of contract

It used to be thought that there were two forms of this tort: the direct form of inducement and the indirect form of inducement. However, the House of Lords unanimously rejected this approach in the case of *OBG Ltd* v *Allan* (2007). The tort of inducement to commit a breach of contract is satisfied in the following scenario:

1. Abdul intentionally induces Brian to commit a breach of his contract with Charles without legal justification, which results in loss to Charles. In such a case, Charles will have a right to sue Abdul in tort. The most common example of the commission of this tort in the industrial context is where a trade union official intentionally persuades an employee member of that trade union to breach his contract of employment with his employer. See Figure 11.3 for a diagrammatical explanation of the tort of inducement to commit a breach of contract. In *OBG Ltd*, the House of Lords clarified that:

2. Abdul must know that he is inducing a breach of contract and that his intentional conduct will have this effect;

3. Charles must show that Abdul intended to induce Brian to commit a breach of contract. If the breach of Brian's contract with Charles is neither an end in itself nor a means to an end, but merely a foreseeable consequence of the actions of Abdul, then Abdul will not have 'intended' to induce Brian to commit a breach of his contract with Charles;

4. this tort imposes secondary or accessory liability on Abdul and requires proof of an actual breach of contract by Brian and thus primary liability on Brian to Charles.

Figure 11.3

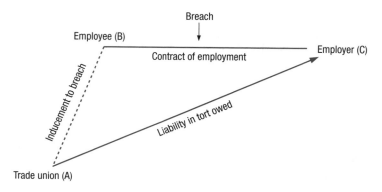

KEY CASE

Lumley v *Gye* [1853] 2 E & B 216

Concerning: inducement to commit a breach of contract

Facts

Miss Wagner had a three-month exclusive contract to sing at Lumley's theatre, which was a rival theatre of the theatre owned by Gye. Gye persuaded Miss Wagner to sing at his theatre for a higher fee than she was being paid by Lumley. Gye was aware of Miss Wagner's existing three-month contract. Lumley sued Gye.

Legal principle

The court held that Gye had committed the tort of inducement in directly inducing Wagner to breach her contract with Lumley.

Causing loss to a third party by unlawful means

In the case of *OBG Ltd*, the House of Lords held that a person will cause loss to a claimant by unlawful means where:

- that person engages in wrongful interference with the liberty of a third party in which the claimant has an economic interest in a way which is unlawful as against that third party;
- that person has an intention thereby to cause loss to the claimant.

Explanation of 'causing loss to a third party by unlawful means'

Consider the following scenario:

1. A is a trade union, e.g. the Allied Electrician's Union;

2. Bruce is the employee of Comfort plc and is a member of the Allied Electrician's Union;

3. Comfort plc are the employers of Bruce;

4. Comfort plc and Dartmouths plc are in contractual relations whereby Comfort plc supply goods or services to Dartmouths plc;

5. The Allied Electrician's Union wishes to cause economic loss to Dartmouths plc.

If an official of the Allied Electrician's Union persuades Bruce to breach his contract of employment with Comfort plc (and thus induce Bruce to incur a loss by breaching his contract with Comfort plc) with a view to ensuring that Comfort plc are unable to service their commercial contract with Dartmouths plc, thus resulting in loss to Dartmouths plc, then the Allied Electrician's Union will be liable in tort to Dartmouths plc, since it has caused loss to Dartmouths plc by unlawful means (see Figure 11.4).

Figure 11.4

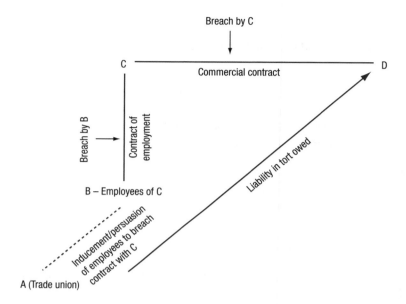

Statutory immunity

Under statute, trade unions are granted certain immunities from tortious liability.

KEY STATUTE

TULRCA 1992, s. 219

(1) An act done by a person in contemplation or furtherance of a trade dispute is not actionable in tort on the ground only –

  (a) that it induces another person to break a contract or interferes or induces another person to interfere with its performance, or

  (b) that it consists in his threatening that a contract (whether one to which he is a party or not) will be broken or its performance interfered with, or that he will induce another person to break a contract or interfere with its performance.

✎ EXAM TIP

You must bear in mind that section 219 of TULRCA 1992 provides immunity from tortious liability only. Hence, contractual liability, criminal liability and other forms of civil liability are not covered. So you should bear this in mind in answering essay questions, and look out for problem questions where you are asked to advise a trade union whether it enjoys immunity in respect of facts which indicate criminal conduct or civil liability which is not tortious. Moreover, the torts in relation to which the trade union enjoys immunity are restricted to the torts specified in the section. So other torts such as breach of statutory duty, harassment and libel are not included within the scope of the immunity.

Section 244 of TULRCA 1992 defines what is meant by **trade dispute** in section 219 of TULRCA above.

KEY DEFINITION: Trade dispute

A dispute between workers and their employer which relates wholly or mainly to one or more of the following:

- terms and conditions of employment;
- engagement or non-engagement, or termination or suspension of employment or the duties of employment, of one or more workers;
- allocation of work or the duties of employment between workers;
- matters of discipline;
- a worker's membership or non-membership of a trade union;
- facilities for officials of trade unions; and
- machinery for negotiation or consultation, including statutory recognition procedures in respect of trade unions.

Exceptions to statutory immunity

There are certain exceptions to the statutory immunity in section 244 of TULRCA 1992. If any of these exceptions are relevant, the trade union does not enjoy the statutory immunity. The exceptions are as follows:

- The statutory immunity of the trade union is removed and industrial action is not protected unless a majority of union members who are likely to be called out to industrial action have consented to such action pursuant to a ballot carried out in accordance with sections 226–235 of TULRCA 1992. The provisions of sections 226–235 of TULRCA 1992 have generated a great deal of case law in recent years, particularly in relation to whether the relevant trade unions concerned had complied with these pre-strike balloting and notice requirements, on which, see *Metrobus Ltd* v *Unite the Union* (2009), *British Airways plc* v *Unite the Union* (2010) and *RMT* v *Serco* (2011).

- If the industrial action is not being taken against the primary employer, the statutory immunity will be removed unless the secondary action is protected secondary action, i.e. lawful picketing falling within section 224 of TULRCA 1992.

■ Putting it all together

Answer guidelines

See the essay question at the start of this chapter. A diagram illustrating how to structure your answer is available on the website.

Approaching the question

The focus in this question is on the economic torts that attract statutory immunities from suit and whether the law is satisfactory. See below for further details.

Important points to include

Points to remember when answering this question:

- Give a brief overview of the main torts in the context of industrial action.
- Explore the scope of the statutory immunities.
- Examine what is not covered by the statutory immunities.

 Make your answer stand out

- Consider whether the statutory immunities are too restricted.

- Place the statutory immunities in their historical, political, economic and social contexts by examining the role of Government in restricting their scope in the past 30 years.

READ TO IMPRESS

Charlwood, A. (2004) The new generation of trade union leaders and prospects for union revitalisation. 42 *British Journal of Industrial Relations*: 379.

Ewing, K. (2005) The function of trade unions. 34 *Industrial Law Journal*: 1.

Ewing, K. and Hendy, J. (2010) The dramatic implications of *Demir and Baykara*. 39 *Industrial Law Journal*: 2.

Simpson, B. (2007) Economic tort liability in labour disputes: the potential impact of the House of Lords' decision in *OBG* v *Allan*. 36 *Industrial Law Journal*: 468.

www.pearsoned.co.uk/lawexpress

 Go online to access more revision support including quizzes to test your knowledge, sample questions with answer guidelines, podcasts you can download, and more!

And finally, before the exam . . .

By using this revision guide to direct your work, you should now have a good knowledge and understanding of the way in which the various aspects of employment law work in isolation and the many ways in which they are interrelated. What is more, you should have acquired the necessary skills and techniques to demonstrate that knowledge and understanding in the exam, regardless of whether the questions are presented to you in essay or problem format. Remember that employment law exams do require you to be accurate and precise. This means that you must be absolutely clear about the point of a case and/or a statutory provision.

Check your progress

☐ Look at the **revision checklists** at the start of each chapter. Are you happy that you can now tick them all? If not, go back to the particular chapter and work through the material again. If you are still struggling, seek help from your tutor.

☐ Attempt the **sample questions** in each chapter and check your answers against the guidelines provided.

☐ Go online to **www.pearsoned.co.uk/lawexpress** for more hands-on revision help:

    ☐ Try the **test your knowledge** quizzes and see if you can score full marks for each chapter.

    ☐ Attempt to answer the **sample questions** for each chapter within the time limit and check your answers against the guidelines provided.

    ☐ Listen to the **podcast** and then attempt the question it discusses.

    ☐ Evaluate sample exam answers in **you be the marker** and see if you can spot their strengths and weaknesses.

    ☐ Use the **flashcards** to test your recall of the legal principles of the key cases and statutes you've revised and the definitions of important terms.

Linking it all up

You should not think of each of the subjects which form part of the area of employment law as discrete self-contained topics with no overlap between each. Check where there are overlaps between subject areas. (You may want to review the 'revision note' boxes throughout this book.) Make a careful note of these as knowing how one topic may lead to another can increase your marks significantly. Here are some examples:

✔ The topic of the statutory national minimum wage overlaps with the statutory right of an employee not to suffer unauthorised deductions from wages, the employer's common law duty to pay the employee for services rendered and the law of equal pay. The reason for this is that each of these laws regulate the wage/work bargain struck between the employer and the employee.

✔ Moreover, there is some overlap between the law of the implied terms of the contract of employment and a number of other employment law topics, e.g. whether an employee has been constructively dismissed often depends on whether there has been a repudiatory breach of one of the implied terms of the contract of employment, such as the implied term of mutual trust and confidence or the implied term that the employer will exercise reasonable care for the employee's physical and psychiatric health.

✔ On a separate note, you should be able to distinguish between a wrongful dismissal, constructive dismissal and an unfair dismissal and the similarities and differences.

Knowing your cases

Make sure you know how to use relevant case law in your answers. Use the table below to focus your revision of the key cases in each topic. To review the details of these cases, refer back to the particular chapter.

Key case	How to use	Related topics
Chapter 1 – The sources and institutions of employment law and key definitions		
Ready Mixed Concrete (South East) Ltd v *Minister of Pensions and National Insurance*	To explain the mechanics of the 'control' test	Distinction between an employee and an independent contractor

Key case	How to use	Related topics
Chapter 1 – The sources and institutions of employment law and key definitions *Continued*		
Montgomery v *Johnson Underwood Ltd*	To show that 'mutuality of obligation' and 'control' represent the irreducible minimum required for the establishment of a contract of employment	Distinction between an employee and an independent contractor
Carmichael and Leese v *National Power plc*	To demonstrate when there is no intention to create an employment relationship	Atypical workers
Mingeley v *Pennock and Ivory t/a Amber Cars*	To demonstrate whether a person is providing a service on the basis of a 'contract personally to do work'	Distinction between an individual providing services as an independent contractor and on the basis of a 'contract personally to do work'
Jivraj v *Hashwani*	To demonstrate whether a person is providing a service on the basis of a 'contract personally to do work'	An individual will only be engaged on the basis of a 'contract personally to do work' if he/she is in a relationship of subordination to the hirer of his/her services, which feature must be a dominant feature of the contract.
Chapter 2 – Implied terms of the contract of employment (1): duties of the employer		
William Hill Organisation Ltd v *Tucker*	To explain the exception to the duty to provide work	Implied term imposing a duty on an employer to provide work
Wilsons & Clyde Coal Co. Ltd v *English*	To demonstrate the employer's implied duty to exercise reasonable care for the physical well-being of its employees	Implied term imposing duty on employer to exercise reasonable care

▶

Key case	How to use	Related topics
Chapter 2 – Implied terms of the contract of employment (1): duties of the employer *Continued*		
Johnstone v *Bloomsbury Health Authority*	To demonstrate how the employer's implied duty to exercise reasonable care for the physical well-being of its employees may control an express term of the employment contract	Implied term imposing duty on employer to exercise reasonable care
Malik v *BCCI SA*	To illustrate a breach of the implied term of the contract of employment that trust and confidence inherent in the employment relationship should be maintained and preserved	Implied term of mutual trust and confidence
Johnson v *Unisys Ltd*	To show that the implied term of mutual trust and confidence is not available to offer additional damages in a wrongful dismissal claim for the manner of an employee's dismissal	Damages for wrongful dismissal (see Chapter 8)
Chapter 3 – Implied terms of the contract of employment (2): duties of the employee		
Pepper v *Webb*	To illustrate a breach of the duty of the employee to follow reasonable and lawful instructions and orders	Implied term imposing a duty on the employee to follow reasonable and lawful instructions and orders
Donovan v *Invicta Airways*	To show circumstances where an employer's instructions or orders are unreasonable or unlawful, thus enabling the employee not to follow them	Exceptions to the implied term imposing a duty on the employee to comply with instructions or orders of the employer

Key case	How to use	Related topics
Chapter 3 – Implied terms of the contract of employment (2): duties of the employee _Continued_		
Lister v _Romford Ice and Cold Storage Co. Ltd_	To explain a breach of the duty of the employee to exercise care	Implied term imposing a duty on the employee to exercise care and perform duties competently
Secretary of State for Employment v _ASLEF_	To show that a 'work to rule' policy was a breach of the duty of the employee to exercise care and perform duties competently	Implied term imposing a duty on the employee to exercise care and perform duties competently
Cresswell v _Board of Inland Revenue_	To show a breach of the implied duty to adapt and cooperate	Implied term imposing a duty on the employee to adapt and cooperate
Briscoe v _Lubrizol Ltd_	To demonstrate a breach of the implied duty of mutual trust and confidence	Implied term of mutual trust and confidence
Item Software (UK) Ltd v _Fassihi_	To explain how senior employees who are fiduciaries are under an implied duty to disclose their own misconduct	Implied term of fidelity imposing an implied duty to disclose own misconduct on senior employees who are fiduciaries
Hivac v _Park Royal Scientific Instruments_	To illustrate a breach of the implied term of fidelity	Implied term of fidelity imposing an implied duty not to work for competitors of the employer or compete with employer
Faccenda Chicken Ltd v _Fowler_	To explain when an employee is not in breach of the implied term of fidelity	Implied term of fidelity imposing an implied duty not to disclose trade secrets subsequent to date of termination of employment ▶

Key case	How to use	Related topics
Chapter 4 – Key statutory employment rights		
Leisure Employment Services Ltd v *Commissioners for HM Revenue & Customs*	To show the calculation of the employer's costs and expenses falling within the 'living accommodation offset' for the purposes of the National Minimum Wage Act 1998	Right to be paid the national minimum wage
SIMAP v *Conselleria de Sanidad y Consumo de la Generalidad Valenciana*	To show how 'time on call' at premises of employer amounts to 'working time'	Meaning of 'working time' under Working Time Regulations 1998
Robinson-Steele v *RD Retail Services Ltd*	To demonstrate 'rolled-up' holiday pay is unlawful	Right to annual leave under Working Time Regulations 1998
Matthews v *Kent and Medway Towns Fire Authority*	To demonstrate the appropriate comparator for a claim by a part-time worker that he/she has been treated less favourably than a full-time worker	Statutory right of part-time workers not to suffer part-time discrimination
Chapter 5 – Discrimination in employment (1)		
James v *Eastleigh Borough Council*	To explain the 'but for' approach to direct discrimination	Direct discrimination
R v *Governing Body of Jews Free School*	Another example of the 'reason why' approach to direct discrimination	Direct discrimination
Jones v *University of Manchester*	To illustrate a comparison exercise under the test of indirect discrimination	Indirect discrimination
Chapter 6 – Discrimination in employment (2)		
Igen Ltd v *Wong*	To explain the operation of the burden of proof in discrimination cases	Burden of proof

Key case	How to use	Related topics
Chapter 6 – Discrimination in employment (2) *Continued*		
Archibald v *Fife Council*	An authority for the proposition that the employer's duty to make reasonable adjustments may entail positive discrimination in favour of a disabled employee	Duty to make reasonable adjustments
Mayor and Burgesses of the London Borough of Lewisham v *Malcolm*	Concerning: the appropriate comparator for 'disability-related discrimination' in s. 3A(1) DDA 1995	Discrimination arising from disability
Chapter 7 – Equal pay		
Capper Pass Ltd v *Lawton*	To show what is meant by the concept of 'like work'	'Like work'
Springboard Sunderland Trust v *Robson*	To show what is meant by the concept of 'work rated as equivalent'	'Work rated as equivalent'
Redcar & Cleveland Borough Council v *Bainbridge*	To show that it is possible for a claimant to compare herself with a higher-paid man if her job is graded with a higher value under a job evaluation study	Job evaluation study
Chapter 8 – Wrongful dismissal		
Malik v *BCCI SA*	Stigma damages are available for a breach of the implied term of mutual trust and confidence as part of a wrongful dismissal action	Stigma damages
Virgin Net Ltd v *Harper*	To demonstrate that damages for loss of opportunity to claim unfair dismissal are not available as part of a wrongful dismissal claim	Damages for wrongful dismissal

▶

Key case	How to use	Related topics
Chapter 9 – Unfair dismissal (1): basic concepts		
Land Securities Trillium Ltd v *Thornley*	repudiatory conduct, constructive dismissal	Constructive dismissal
British Home Stores Ltd v *Burchell*	To explain the 'range of reasonable responses' test and the approach to be applied in the case of the misconduct of an employee	Range of reasonable responses test
Polkey v *AE Dayton Services Ltd*	To show that the 'no difference' argument is not available to an employer	Fair and proper procedure
Chapter 10 – Unfair dismissal (2): remedies and redundancy		
Murray v *Foyle Meats Ltd*	To explain the authority for causation approach to 'work of a particular kind'	Redundancy
Chapter 11 – Collective labour law		
Lumley v *Gye*	To show when a person will have induced another to commit a breach of contract	Inducement of another to commit a breach of contract

■ Sample question

Below is an essay question that incorporates overlapping areas of the law. See if you can answer this question drawing upon your knowledge of the whole subject area. Guidelines on answering this question are included at the end of this section.

ESSAY QUESTION

To what extent has the concept of constructive dismissal been central to the evolution of the implied term of mutual trust and confidence?

Answer guidelines

Approaching the question

You should begin your answer to the above question by noting that 'constructive dismissal' is a statutory concept recognised by statute in terms of section 95(1)(c) of the Employment Rights Act 1996. Meanwhile, the implied term of mutual trust and confidence is a common law concept, i.e. a term of the contract of employment which was developed by the courts incrementally over time in a series of cases.

Important points to include

Section 95(1)(c) of the Employment Rights Act 1996 refers to conduct on the part of the employer which is such that the employee is entitled to terminate the contract of employment without notice. In the case of *Western Excavating (ECC) Ltd* v *Sharp* (1978), it was held that whether the employer's conduct was reasonable or unreasonable was not the appropriate test for determining whether an employee had been constructively dismissed. Instead, the question was whether the employer's conduct:

- amounted to a significant or repudiatory breach of contract going to the root of the contract of employment; or
- demonstrated that the employer no longer intended to be bound by one or more of the essential terms of the contract.

Against that backdrop, the Employment Appeal Tribunal and the courts developed the content and scope of the implied term of mutual trust and confidence to give clearer content to what would amount to a repudiatory breach on the part of the employer. The law evolved to the point that where there is conduct on the part of the employer which demonstrates that trust and confidence between it and the employee has broken down or has been severely undermined, this will be treated as a significant or repudiatory breach of contract going to the root of the contract of employment (see *Morrow* v *Safeway Stores plc* (2002)). Thus, an employee subjected to such treatment will be deemed to have been constructively dismissed. To that extent, the statutory innovation of 'constructive dismissal' is primarily responsible for the development of this implied term. For further discussion of this point, see the speech of Lord Nicholls in *Eastwood* v *Magnox Electric plc* (2004) at Paras. [6]–[16].

 Make your answer stand out

Consider whether any elements of the common law of the implied term of mutual trust and confidence have developed in isolation from the law of constructive dismissal.

■ Further practice

To test yourself further, try to answer these three questions, which also incorporate overlapping areas of the law. Evaluate your answers using the answer guidelines available on the companion website at **www.pearsoned.co.uk/lawexpress**

Question 1

'The main object of labour law has always been, and we venture to say will always be, to be a countervailing force to counteract the inequality of bargaining power which is inherent and must be inherent in the employment relationship.'

In light of this statement, how well does British Labour Law protect employees and workers?

Question 2

Keira has been employed for the last three years as a customer sales advisor for a mobile phone company. She is called into her supervisor's office and is told that a random check by the IT department has revealed that she has been accessing anti-abortion websites during her lunch breaks. The staff handbook states that computer access that is not work-related constitutes gross misconduct. Keira indignantly protests that this practice of surfing the web is commonplace and that the supervisors were aware that it was common practice and did not mind, provided it only happened during lunch breaks. However, her supervisor ignores her protests and threatens to give her a final written warning. Keira is appalled by this revelation, and gets up and walks out of the employer's premises never to return to work.

Under the terms of her employment contract Keira is entitled to two months' notice, but does not receive payment in lieu of such notice after she walks out. Keira's employers are angry because Keira has told lots of people that she has been badly treated. Her employers make it known that the reason for Keira's summary dismissal was because she was accessing anti-abortion websites. Keira, who is clearly upset by her former employer's conduct, has come to you for advice about her rights.

Advise Keira.

Question 3

Jane has been working for 'Bake-a-dat-Cake' for 14 years. She usually works a standard 35-hour week. However, six months ago, two members of staff left 'Bake-a-dat-Cake' and Mrs Cupcake, the owner, did not replace them. Instead, she told the remaining staff that they would have to work harder and longer hours to compensate for the reduced number of employees. For the last four months, Jane has been working around 55 hours each week and she is getting to the point where she is completely exhausted and feels that she is going to end up having a breakdown due to overwork. Jane has told Mrs Cupcake about her deteriorating health, but Mrs Cupcake has told her to get on with it.

Jane's aged mother, who lives with Jane, has been in a car accident and has broken her leg and cannot walk. Jane has told Mrs Cupcake that she will have to take a couple of days off work to care for her mother and to arrange for neighbours and friends to look in regularly to check that her mother is okay. Mrs Cupcake said that she is under no legal duty to pay Jane while she is off. Mrs Cupcake said that she doesn't pay pregnant staff when they attend ante-natal appointments, so she doesn't see why she should pay Jane when there's nothing wrong with her. Jane takes a total of six days off during a two month period to look after her mother. She is not paid for those six days.

Jane is furious about this failure to pay, so storms into the bakery one day and tells Mrs Cupcake that she is going to hand in her notice and look for a job in another bakery. Mrs Cupcake responds by berating Jane in front of customers in the bakery, criticising her dress sense and her standard of work. Jane is deeply affected by this public humiliation and soon develops a psychiatric illness that necessitates her to take a substantial period of time off work. Mrs Cupcake is unsympathetic and after two months of Jane being absent from work because of sickness, Mrs Cupcake decides to dismiss Jane without any payment in lieu of notice or payment in lieu of untaken holidays: when Jane was dismissed, it was nine months into the holiday year, and Jane had taken no annual leave.

Advise Jane.

Glossary of terms

The glossary is divided into two parts: key definitions and other useful terms. The key definitions can be found within the chapter in which they occur, as well as in the glossary below. These definitions are the essential terms that you must know and understand in order to prepare for an exam. The additional list of terms provides further definitions of useful terms and phrases which will also help you answer examination and coursework questions effectively. These terms are highlighted in the text as they occur but the definition can only be found here.

▣ Key definitions

Fixed-term contract	A contract which endures for a specific period of time and terminates at the end of that period of time.
Implied term of mutual trust and confidence	A term of the contract of employment that each party will not, without reasonable and proper cause, act in such a way as would be calculated or likely to destroy or seriously damage the relationship of trust and confidence existing between it and the other party to the contract.
Independent trade union	A trade union which is not under the domination or control of an employer, group of employers or employers' association and is not liable to interference by an employer (arising out of the provision of financial or material support or by any other means whatsoever) tending towards such control.
Industrial action	Action taken by members of a trade union that imposes restrictions upon employers when collective relations between the employer and the workforce break down.
Repudiatory breach of contract	A breach of a term of a contract which goes to the root of that contract so that on the occurrence of breach the innocent party may be regarded as discharged from further performance of his or her obligations under the contract.

Trade dispute

A dispute between workers and their employer which relates wholly or mainly to one or more of the following:

- terms and conditions of employment;
- engagement or non-engagement, or termination or suspension of employment or the duties of employment, of one or more workers;
- allocation of work or the duties of employment between workers;
- matters of discipline;
- a worker's membership or non-membership of a trade union;
- facilities for officials of trade unions;
- machinery for negotiation or consultation, including statutory recognition procedures in respect of trade unions.

Unfair dismissal

The dismissal of an employee which is unfair in terms of Part X of the Employment Rights Act 1996.

Wrongful dismissal

The dismissal of an employee which amounts to a repudiatory breach of contract on the part of the employer.

■ Other useful terms

Constructive dismissal

Where an employee terminates the contract under which he or she is employed (with or without notice) in circumstances in which he or she is entitled to terminate it without notice by reason of the employer's conduct.

Disability

Where a person has a physical or mental impairment which has a substantial and long-term adverse effect on his or her ability to carry out normal day-to-day activities.

Employee

An individual who has entered into or works under a contract of employment.

Redundancy

Where an employee's dismissal is wholly or mainly attributable to –

a. the fact that his or her employer has ceased or intends to cease –

   i.   to carry on the business for the purposes of which the employee was employed by it, or

   ii. to carry on that business in the place where the employee was so employed, or

b. the fact that the requirements of that business –

    i. for employees to carry out work of a particular kind, or

    ii. for employees to carry out work of a particular kind in the place where the employee was employed by the employer,

have ceased or diminished or are expected to cease or diminish.

Trade union An organisation which consists wholly or mainly of workers of one or more descriptions and whose principal purposes include the regulation of relations between workers of that description or those descriptions and employers or employers' associations.

Worker An individual who has entered into or works under (a) a contract of employment, or (b) any other contract, whereby the individual undertakes to do or perform personally any work or services for another party to the contract whose status is not by virtue of the contract that of a client or customer of any profession or business undertaking carried on by the individual.

Index

Note: A page number in **bold** refers to a glossary entry.

INDEX